# FORTY YEARS SIXTEEN DAYS

PENNINE WAY

# FORTY YEARS SIXTEEN DAYS

Chris Priest and Duncan Say

First published by Sleight Books in 2022


A catalogue record of this book is available from the British Library.
ISBN - 978-1-916217-2-3 paperback
ISBN - 978-1-916217-3-0 eBook

Also available:
Masked - the unbelievable Harry Bensley
by
Duncan Say

Front cover photos: 'Walking down to Dufton from High Cup'
mashed with 'Rainbow over Middleton-in-Teesdale'

Do not lead for I will not follow.

Do not follow for I will not lead.

Just walk with me and be my friend.

*Anon.*

The route of the Pennine Way

# CONTENTS

*To*
*Mag and Sylvie*

# High Cup

**Chris:** The late afternoon September sunshine warmed us as we climbed from Maize Beck to the level ground of High Cup Plain. It was not a particularly demanding ascent and having already covered sixteen of Day 10's twenty miles from Middleton-in-Teesdale, we felt no need to hurry. As the ground flattened out, the path coincided with the course of a shallow stream which we followed until ahead of us we could see it suddenly took a steep downward turn. We watched the sparkling water disappear over a rocky edge, beyond which we glimpsed the distant precipitous wall of the far side of a deep valley. But then, walking just a few steps further we were assailed by the full magnificence of the breath-taking, stand out moment of the Pennine Way.

## *High Cup*

The scale, the symmetry, the perfection of High Cup, revealed as we reached the edge and took in the full panorama, simply blew us away. The view along this textbook glaciated valley was enhanced, if that was possible, by the low afternoon sunshine, picking out in sharp contrast the craggy outcrops lining the sides.

Glistening in the valley bottom, the silvery ribbon of High Cup Gill Beck hinted at the depth of this remarkable natural feature. We could only sit and stare in silence, for minutes on end.

Amazing that we were so affected really, when you consider that it wasn't the first time we'd been there.

**The scale, symmetry and perfection of High Cup**

'What?'

# Chapter 1

**Duncan:** I suppose it's not regarded as normal behaviour to want to walk the Pennine Way once, let alone twice. So how did it come about? I don't believe that either of us can point at one particular moment that drew us here. It must have grown organically, in much the same way as our lasting friendship which began over forty five years ago when we moved into a student house while we were at Poly. We were both studying photography and spent the final year in a house in Leytonstone, in London's east end. As student days ended eventually we moved apart to pursue our fledgling careers but we kept in touch. Coming together with our friends to play football, party and much more, but we never went walking. The threads of that go back much further still.

**Chris**: For me, growing up in the east midlands, childhood trips to the Peak District were fairly common and on one school trip we were bussed to Edale to walk what approximated to the first half day of the Pennine Way. I enjoyed such outings immensely but wouldn't claim they were the start of a lifetime passion for hillwalking. Nevertheless, sometime between autumn 1977 and Easter 1979 the plan to tackle the two hundred and seventy mile marathon of the Pennine Way was hatched. Pinning down the time of this decision more precisely than that is difficult, for me at least. Duncan has suggested that the seed of the idea was perhaps planted by BBC TV's 'Go with Noakes'. In one episode, the much-loved Blue Peter star tackled the Pennine Way. Records show though that the programme aired in March 1977, too early I think to have been the inspiration.

**Duncan**: Although the countryside was miles away from my south London home, my parents had lifetime membership of the Scottish Youth Hostel Association and we would often as a family head out hosteling. Being six years younger than my sister, I was always the straggler on these walks. Of an evening in the youth hostel common room the real walkers would sit, generally in a pool of water, or more

often in the fug of pipe-smoke. (I could be challenged on this as smoking probably wasn't allowed in youth hostels.) They would tell loud and boastful tales of indomitable endurance, in between singing folk songs. Yes it really was that bad and I knew, even as a ten year old, that I was not of that ilk.

**Straggling on King's Seat, Perthshire.**

A few years later we moved to Coventry and during sixth form at school some of my classmates decided that they wanted to walk the Pennine Way. To our amazement, the old fossil who used to take us for biology was very enthused by these plans and we found that we could easily distract him by getting him to talk about hill walking. The mention of an unusual insect-eating plant being found in peat bogs was enough to set him off on a tangential monologue for up to forty minutes, which we would gleefully time.

Later I probably saw the 'Go with Noakes' programme with Chris when we were living in the student house. Being students, watching children's tv on the rented black and white television was what you did. For example, on a Saturday morning 'Tiswas' followed by a lunch of takeaway pie, mash and liquor was the beginning of a great weekend. We liked to live large in Leytonstone in those days.

We might have forgotten about the programme but I do remember that for the first two summers after leaving college I didn't have a holiday, mainly because working as a photographic assistant I barely had enough money to pay the rent and eat. As the next summer approached we both felt that we needed a proper break and must have begun to think of a cheap way to fill the days.

**Chris:** Anyway, perhaps the more interesting question is why did we decide to do it? What did we think we'd get out of it? Was it just something to do in the holidays? There'd certainly be a sense of achievement on completion, though I'm sure I never felt that I somehow needed to test myself. We knew it would be tough, but as long as we prepared sensibly there'd be no reason why a couple of healthy twenty-somethings couldn't walk fifteen to twenty miles every day for a fortnight. Through peat bogs in the rain. Carrying a tent that we'd sleep in overnight.

I knew nobody else who'd done it, or was intending to do it, so there was no sense of competition or needing to follow in the footsteps of others. I think that the main motivator was just enjoyment – we thought we'd have a good time. It would be good fun and a great experience.

**Duncan:** We broke in our boots walking along the towpath of the River Lea which offered an unambiguous route for us novice navigators. The starting point was the Prince of Wales pub on Lea Bridge Road, in east London (which has transitioned to the Princess of Wales in the interim years). It was an old fashioned Young's pub filled with crusty locals and real ale drinkers. We were mysteriously aware that Waltham Abbey was ten miles to the north and so there and back would be a proper test of our abilities. We completed this walk many times but soon felt a need to widen our horizons. In the local library we found a slim booklet of walks by the West Essex Ramblers Association.

The first walks we tried were through Epping Forest and they normally ended up at an underground station that could take us home. As the weeks went by we explored further.

A particular favourite was a walk between Epping station and Chipping Ongar, then the furthest flung outpost of the Central line. Along the route we drank in a lonely McMullens pub, the Moletrap at Tawney Common. On one walk, in a field beyond this pub, we had a close encounter with a large herd of bullocks causing us to leg it across a field and vault a stile to safety. (Those bullocks were 'only curious' as the daughter of a farmer laughingly informed us.)

**Chris:** I remember the time we arrived at Ongar underground station at the start of a walk, the day after a television wildlife programme had featured a colony of a rare species of scorpion which bizarrely had established itself on the station. As the train doors slid open, a bunch of people rose from their seats clutching Tupperware boxes and headed to the undergrowth at the edge of the platform where they started searching for the unsuspecting arachnids. On another weekend we even, inexplicably, did a walk through Epping Forest at night. As dawn broke, we were to be found snoozing in a bus shelter at the Wake Arms roundabout on the A11.

**Duncan:** The night walk through the forest was a one-off because it was a little worrying when we stumbled across some people in the darkness emptying a large object from a car boot. Not wishing to be the next objects to be dragged off into the forest we kept well out of sight.

The West Essex Ramblers had brought out a series of books and they were all remarkably well written (for what was basically instruction). They did include the classic line 'turn left, then right, i.e., straight on,' quite often, which we would chant out when it occurred in the text. However, it all made sense when we were out on the fields and we rarely got lost. The authors, Fred Matthews and Harry Bitten's love of the Essex countryside shone through every page.

**Chris:** We realised that to go from these gentle Sunday walks to the gruelling two hundred and seventy miles of the Pennine Way would need further preparation, and so to establish a baseline, a mission to walk the first two or three days of the Way was undertaken, over the Easter weekend of 1979.

We gathered much from this trip, principally that there was a reason why flared denims were not *de rigueur* for walkers. It was evident too that we would definitely need to get many more miles under our belts to be really up to the challenge and crucially, we learned that only an idiot attempts the Pennine Way with several days worth of tinned food in his rucksack. The need to travel light was impressed upon us when one shoulder strap of my rucksack decided to object to this extreme burden by tearing away from the body of the sack as we crossed Kinder Scout; lesson very clearly learned.

**Flares are not *de rigueur* for walkers**

**Duncan:** And reinforced by that guy who spoke to us in the Lion in Ripponden.

'You walking the Pennine Way?'

It was a surprise to be addressed by a gnarled walker (he was probably ten years older than us and therefore extremely ancient in our eyes).

'Practising,' we replied.

We had tried to walk the first section from Edale and had found it very challenging indeed. Although the weather was warm we encountered deep drifts of snow on the hills. After a couple of days floundering across snow filled peat bog we had decided to make our way to the nearby town and reassess our prospects. Inside the pub, Dire

**Duncan is *à la mode* in his mum's Fair Isle knitwear**

Straits was on the jukebox and Mark Knopfler was singing 'the Sultans of Swing' when this bearded specimen had deigned to talk to us.

'Your packs?' He nodded at our bursting rucksacks resting beside the bentwood chairs (Chris's pack had fallen apart by this stage).

'Yes.'

'How much do they weigh?'

We exchanged bemused looks because we hadn't the foggiest idea. Our theory, if you could call it that was if you could fit it in you could carry it. After all, that's what a backpack was for.

'No more than twenty five pounds, you won't make it otherwise,' he commented dryly before returning to his beer.

Our packs were full of vital supplies for a bank holiday weekend and when we got back home and weighed them they were each over forty pounds. How on earth were we going to slim them down? It was only later that we were to learn that real walkers have - *how can I say this politely?* - a more relaxed attitude to personal hygiene.

**Chris:** From then until late August, most Sundays and occasionally long weekends were given over to walking. We trod many miles during the spring and summer months, becoming very familiar with Epping Forest, the Lea Valley and those bits of Essex accessible from the Central Line. Confidence in our ability to walk a long way and for many hours grew, but we knew also that the paths of eastern England lacked one thing that we really needed to test ourselves against - hills. We would only find out if we were really up to the Pennine Way when we got there.

**Duncan:** In the following weeks while we were out practising, sometimes at a field edge that lacked a stile, or a stream without a crossing, the instructions would stop making sense and it was at this moment that the map and compass would come out. We would scan the horizon for obvious markers, maybe a church steeple to the north west, a water tower to the east and from these try and work out where we were using the art of trigonometry. I say art, as in my hands it definitely was not a science.

Either we were not very good at it or the Essex countryside was filled with similar looking landmarks. We could be lost for up to an hour at a time as we mistook one place for another, until we finally stumbled across a church notice board, or a road junction that conclusively placed us on the map.

By this stage we were both employed at Bart's Hospital in London and at lunchtimes would get together and visit specialist walking and mountaineering shops. Opposite the Old Bailey was the Scout Shop, a tiny space that held a small display of gear suitable for outdoor types. It was here that we both bought our walking trousers.

State of the art trousers in 1979 meant something heavy and woollen. There was one style which was ankle length and a second that ended just below the knee. However the Scout Shop held limited stock or maybe the crofter and loom were taking a break, and although I admired the longer trouser it had already sold out in my waist size leaving me with no option but to buy the 'plus twos'. This was the kind of trouser that is only worn by investment bankers on a shooting weekend as such garments are regarded by walkers these days as totally ridiculous and utterly impractical.

**Plus Twos, someone must love them**

**Chris:** A bit further away from the hospital in Holborn there were some bigger outdoor stores, notably Black's, said at the time to be 'of Greenock' and Ellis Brigham. It was to Black's that we headed to investigate tents and found several on display, actually nailed down, it being impossible to peg them out on the wooden floor. We eventually decided on the shared purchase of a two-man option. It had a reasonable sized sleeping compartment and a 'porch' in which we could fire up the stove, and was a weight that shared between us, would be very comfortable to carry.

We were not seasoned campers and knew we needed to learn how to erect the tent before venturing out in the Pennines, but we had not a square foot of garden between us, so where could we do that? Well - obviously - in the middle of the Robin Hood roundabout on the A11. Off we went to Epping Forest on a pleasant Sunday lunch time, and after several pints of the finest Courage Directors the Robin Hood had to offer, with the help of various friends and supporters up the tent went, amidst the hooting and shouted comments of passing motorists. Ee, the things you do when you're young.

**The Robin Hood roundabout on the A11 (sadly) without the tent**

**Duncan:** Slowly we accumulated the equipment; lightweight sleeping bags, a gas burner, a saucepan set that doubled as plates, at the same time we were reducing the weight we would carry.

**Chris:** As the big trip loomed we even took to walking to and from work every day (about four miles each way for me) to get the miles in. We were taking this seriously.

**Duncan:** For me it was about eight miles. Leaving at six in the morning and in the evening I would be home by seven thirty. At lunchtimes I would take to the stairs, walking up and down the twelve stories of the office block I worked in. My colleagues must have thought I was mad.

**Chris:** When the time came, we felt sure that we'd practised enough and would certainly be able to give the Way a good go. We headed north to stay overnight at my family home in Worksop, and then next day - the 19th of August - my parents drove us the thirty odd miles to Edale. We felt good and confident of success.

**It's a sign**

**The 'boys' in Slovakia, L to R Andy, Chris, Bill, Jerome & Duncan**

# Chapter 2

**Chris**: And now, all these years later, we had decided to do it again and, once again, the obvious question is why. There are definitely sections of the Pennine Way that are fairly unpleasant even in good conditions and having completed it once, why would anybody submit themselves to such experiences again? Rose tinted glasses maybe; just remembering the good bits? I had certainly begun to crave the opportunity to once again be on those moors and in the Pennine landscape. Duncan and I had walked all over Europe in recent years with our walking buddies, 'the boys' and had fantastic experiences in Spain, France, Greece, Slovakia and Italy but the walking was always just for the day. The Pennine Way though is a journey: to actually walk *somewhere*, not just in a circle and back home for tea really called to me.

I had first drifted the idea to Duncan perhaps as far back as 2015. He says now that he had his doubts and that he thought if we were to undertake such a mission, why not go somewhere we hadn't been before. Or even make a second attempt on the Offa's Dyke path which we'd failed miserably to complete in 1980. He didn't dismiss the idea out of hand but I suppose I went quiet on it for a while, mainly because I realised that it would be very difficult to magic the three weeks away from work and family that would be necessary. I was one of two directors of a company whose twenty or so employees provided photographic services under contract to the NHS. I was responsible for the day to day delivery of those services and as the 2010s wore on my job was getting harder and harder, keeping me busy for substantially more than forty hours a week. Having had the great idea to revisit the Way, at the time it just wasn't realisable.

In 2017, work changed dramatically when my business partner and I decided that the time was right to opt for an easier life and in May of that year we closed the company. A few months later, capitalising on the time that was now more readily available, Duncan and I started meeting on Thursdays to walk in Essex or Suffolk, in the space between our homes at opposite corners of Essex.

During one of these walks I raised again the subject of a Pennine Way reprise. This time the idea gestated with Duncan until in May 2018, while we were on one of our annual walking trips to foreign lands, he agreed that we should definitely tackle the Way again and that it would be brilliant to do so the following year, the fortieth anniversary of our first outing. Not only that, but we should write a book about it! The last bit was a tall order for me having never attempted 'writing' before, but I knew Duncan was enjoying the creation of his first book, *Masked – the unbelievable Harry Bensley* and couldn't avoid being swept along with his enthusiasm for the idea.

Launching the plan in Spain where we were enjoying the Sierra Nevada with boys Jerome, Bill and Steve gave us a great opportunity to subject our intentions to peer review. Where our 1979 audience had been sceptical, the boys - perhaps not surprisingly - were massively supportive. They thought it was a great idea and were sure that we'd be capable of completing it.

On our return home our wives generously agreed to the plan despite the requirement for three weeks away. It wasn't just the time – a fair amount of cash would need to be spent too – but I think they both saw that this was something we really wanted to do and were also supportive. My wife, Mag, thought that writing about it was a good idea too.

**Duncan:** Although we had brought up the idea of walking the Way nearly a year earlier, it wasn't until 28th February 2019 that it became real. The thought of retracing our steps along the long-distance footpath was one of the motivations for continuing our Thursday walks and they became longer and more challenging as the year went on. That day was the first time that we actually began to discuss how we would approach the walk.

To be physically able to walk the Pennine Way is but one requirement. Where to sleep, how to eat, what to carry, where to stop?

These are questions we barely bothered asking forty years ago, because then we had a tent, some dried food and YHA membership. As twenty-three year olds we thought we had covered all eventualities in our planning to walk the Way.

How would we approach these issues today? Youth hostels are less common than they used to be and get booked up long in advance. Neither of us were keen on taking a tent and as for dried food, no thank you.

One answer is companies that will move luggage from one resting place to the next and even book the accommodation and all the meals along the Way. This service comes at a price, amounts adjacent to the cost of an exotic holiday, but the comments on their websites suggest that this is a popular approach.

We were sceptical that this would work for us, mainly because our experience of walking the Pennine Way had showed us that the weather can play havoc with a plan (like when the River Aire flooded the path). Also we had to consider our physical health as aches and pains are more common for us oldies. Finally the high cost was difficult to justify to ourselves let alone to our families.

**Name: River Aire**
**Hobbies: Flooding, potholing and playing havoc with walkers**

We reluctantly agreed that we should carry tents as that would give us the freedom to pitch anywhere. It also meant that we would have to carry packs unless we could persuade our walking friends to be our support network along the Way. To reduce the weight we decided that we would not cook in the belief that pubs and restaurants would be more readily available than forty years ago. Having made all these decisions there was a list of equipment to be found. For me, a rucksack, a tent, a sleeping bag and a sleeping pad.

**Chris:** The same was true for me. With the exception of boots and socks, all the walking gear I owned was more suited to the single day walking we'd been doing in the more predictably warm and dry climes of Spain. For northern England we'd need clothing that was more dedicated to keeping us dry. Then around April my boots, which were of the Gore-Tex panel variety, sprang a leak. This type of boot with its many seams must always be vulnerable to such failure it seems to me, so a replacement pair with an upper constructed of a single piece of leather went on the list. Thinking that new boots might need to be worn in, a nice pair of Scarpas was bought and pushed immediately into action. I needn't have worried though: unlike the painfully inflexible things I'd bought in 1979 these modern boots were superbly comfortable and felt 'worn in' from the off.

The cost of all this stuff is not low. Having splashed out on the boots I could see as I researched the other things I needed that it was going to cost hundreds of pounds to be properly clothed and equipped. I resolved to get busy flogging off some old photographic equipment to help fund the enterprise. Mostly film cameras, this gear had been gathered over my five decades of involvement with photography, and happily proved surprisingly popular with the eBay community.

Around this time I read online that a high proportion of Pennine Way starters, despite being well equipped, head home after only a couple of days. Many of these people apparently turn up, sporting all the state of the art clothing and equipment that the market has to offer, but lacking a fundamental understanding of walking and the hills. Characterised and derided as having 'all the gear, no idea', they simply can't hack Kinder, Bleaklow and Black Hill. As I made my purchases, I wondered if that's how Duncan and I would appear as we stepped out at Edale, clad in and carrying all our shiny new purchases. Well, we couldn't avoid having new stuff and of course we'd buy the best we could afford – we'd just have to make sure we lasted more than three days.

**Duncan:** There was another problem for me to face and one that no amount of planning could overcome.

Thirty years ago I developed a spasm in my neck after playing football. Some years later an X-ray showed that my sacrum and first lumbar vertebra were fused and my second lumbar vertebra was strangely deformed. It was proposed that these deformities were the cause of a lack of curvature at the bottom of the spine and as a consequence my neck was working hard to compensate.

The diagnosis alarmingly was *Spina Bifida Occulta* which sounds much worse than it is. *Occulta* means hidden and some sufferers are unaware that they have any problem at all. However the following decade was terrible with me resorting to manipulation, medication and massage to try and control the pain. I had to give up many activities including walking.

I will be forever grateful to a neighbour who recommended a therapist who would be regarded as a quack by both mainstream and alternative practitioners. However by this time I was desperate for a different approach. She had started her practice after she recovered from a serious motorcycle accident in Germany. The surgeons saved her life but her back was severely damaged. She then embarked on her own journey of discovery to overcome her back problems. Her suggestions for me were some unusual exercises and a weird machine that she referred to as a 'Nordic Massager' which pummelled the entire length of my spine. In just six, monthly consultations she changed my life.

I ended the sessions physically stronger but more importantly with a completely different mental attitude to my problem. I now understood that although I will never be able to fully repair my back, only I can take the steps to manage it. Within a year I was walking the Inca trail in Peru, something that I would have regarded as a pipe dream before I met her.

**At Dead Woman's Pass on the Inca trail**

Today I am mercifully free of the worst pains but that does not mean to say that I can do what I want. I have to take reasonable care, which for me means practising Tai chi and having a range of massaging aids. The machines are all fabulous but they can't come with me. Added to this, the prospect of carrying a twenty-five pound pack was not one that I was entirely comfortable with, as just carrying a day-pack can tighten up my back muscles.

Despite my misgivings the next piece of the jigsaw was the rucksack and after looking online and reading barely credible reviews about how comfortable rucksacks are, I spent a couple of hours in a large camping superstore trying on various makes. This was a revelation. Even the cheapest rucksack was streets ahead in terms of comfort to the sheer horror of my previous experience. Back then, putting the rucksack on in the morning was the worst moment of a walking day, as the aches and pains from the bare straps started the moment the sack was in position.

In looking for a rucksack I had several criteria. I wanted it to be well ventilated, I wanted it to be adaptable, so that I could make fine adjustments to find the best carrying position for me. Finally, I wanted it to be as comfortable as possible so that my back would be less likely to spasm.

After an hour or so of trying on various makes there was one rucksack that was markedly better than the rest. Of course, it came with a price tag to match. I made my excuses and left but it nagged away at me. I went online and read reviews about it and my brief experience in the shop was confirmed by experienced walkers. This sack was worth the money, especially in my case, so I bought it.

In April a group of us travelled up to Staffordshire to stay at the newly built house of Jonathan, one of our walking friends. It had taken him eighteen years to design and construct out of stone and oak and was now beautifully set in the rolling countryside. Sitting in his kitchen eating bacon sandwiches with the band of walkers, the conversation drifted around to the Pennine Way. It was time to flesh out our plans and I could tell as the details spilled out that there was a certain scepticism amongst our companions about having a tent and carrying a rucksack. I can understand why. Given the choice, who would not want a cosy bed for the night and a lightweight day-pack filled merely with essentials? To spurn such a sensible course seems wilfully spartan. We press the idea that we are merely being practical because when walking there will be unexpected moments and flexibility is key.

Just a month later we travelled as a group to the Vikos Gorge in Greece. Because of their remoteness the mountain villages of Zagori escaped the attention of the Ottoman invaders and became self-sufficient by building an extraordinary set of well maintained paths between them.

**Steve and Bill sit on the edge of the 3000 ft deep Vikos Gorge**

The walking was unusual in that the day started with a long walk down and ended with a significant ascent. This was an opportunity to see just how much difference the last year had made to our fitness and we were both pleasantly surprised to suffer no ill effects.

Maybe we won't have any problems on the Way, after all.

**Chris:** Apart from the boot purchase, I was some way behind Duncan in my preparations, conforming to my typically last minute way of dealing with things. As I've found to be the case many times over the years, Duncan's research is usually thorough and his conclusions reliable, so we ended up with a lot of the same kit. I had the advantage of being able to try his rucksack before I had to buy, and having had the opportunity to carry it around Essex, I imaginatively bought the same one. We also left for Edale equipped with the same solar powered battery charger and inflatable sleeping mat, among other matching things. One thing I had researched myself was tents and had been amazed to see how light the modern hi-tech fabrics made the tents that were on offer. On-line reviews pointed me at the Vango Helium which weighed in at a mere 1.2kg, but there were any number on the market of similar specification. I bought it and put it up once a few days before we left and I have to say I was fairly baffled by the internal tensioning cords that seemed to block the entry. Perhaps I did something wrong, but I'd run out of time to practice so I put that to the back of my mind, where it shared space with the thought that I was being too optimistic in investing in a two season sleeping bag. (It turned out I was!)

With slightly more urgency I did embark upon the creation of a spreadsheet (that sounds like part of a tent - an *Excel* spreadsheet) detailing the accommodation and catering opportunities to be found on each stage. First I created route maps using the Ordnance Survey app, defining start and stop points for each day. Perhaps not surprisingly these matched almost exactly those from 1979 – the geography of the Pennine Way does tend to impose itself on the progress of those who walk at a normal speed. Then I tried to match stop points with our preferred accommodation option, a youth hostel, but I learned from the YHA website that not only are there fewer hostels now, but the ones that are still open were fully booked for the days we needed. So then I identified campsites, and as we had decided not to carry food, where we'd be able to eat. Evening meal sources were generally easy to identify as there's usually a pub somewhere nearby, but finding breakfasting opportunities was trickier. With a few days to go the spreadsheet was pretty much complete - just a couple of ominous empty cells - and imagining it would see plenty of use, I printed and laminated copies for us both to carry.

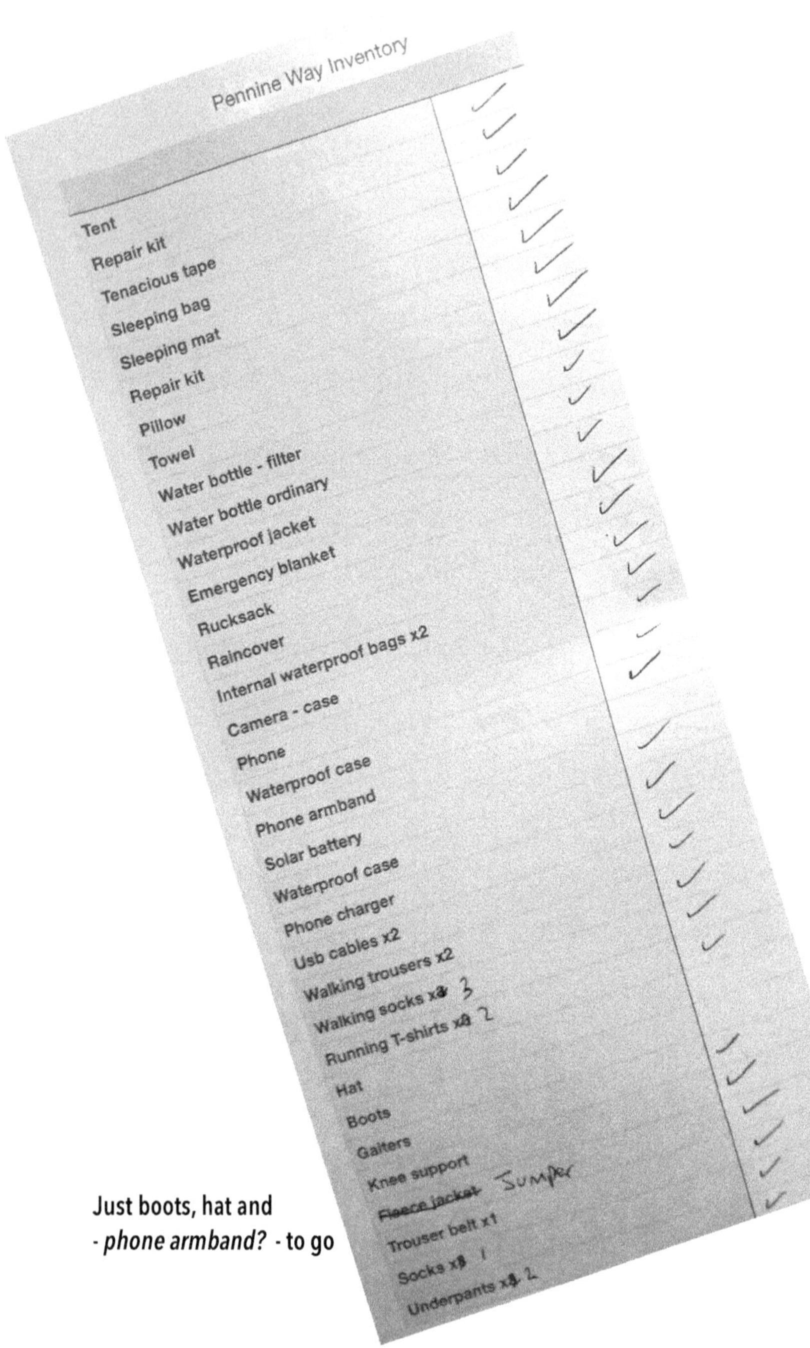
Pennine Way Inventory

Tent
Repair kit
Tenacious tape
Sleeping bag
Sleeping mat
Repair kit
Pillow
Towel
Water bottle - filter
Water bottle ordinary
Waterproof jacket
Emergency blanket
Rucksack
Raincover
Internal waterproof bags x2
Camera - case
Phone
Waterproof case
Phone armband
Solar battery
Waterproof case
Phone charger
Usb cables x2
Walking trousers x2
Walking socks x3 3
Running T-shirts x3 2
Hat
Boots
Gaiters
Knee support
~~Fleece jacket~~ Jumper
Trouser belt x1
Socks x3 1
Underpants x3 2

Just boots, hat and
- *phone armband?* - to go

# Chapter 3

**Duncan:** Whittling down the items to pack took me several days and much heart searching. I began like a proper grown-up with an inventory of essentials that I'd spent weeks compiling. Normally when packing for a holiday I would avoid such pre-planning, throwing items together at the last minute but on this occasion decisions have to be made. Some of these, such as the final number of pants and socks will only be determined once the pack has been weighed.

I followed the inventory to the letter as each item had by now some element of necessity. Breezily I put in a lightweight jumper and shorts for evening wear and then shouldered the backpack. The scales told an alarming story of being seven pounds over the target weight of twenty-five pounds. Seven pounds is a significant amount, similar to the average weight of a domestic wash. Never mind the evening wear, lurking inside the backpack were items which I'd already deemed essential that now will have to pass a meaner test.

I emptied my pack and looked over the pile. To find out what I needed to achieve I repacked the indispensable items first. The tent, sleeping bag, the sleeping mat, inflatable pillow, and a towel. A first aid kit, toiletries, drugs and toothbrush. A toilet roll. Compass, head torch and tools to repair the tent. Lightweight shoes, hat, waterproof jacket and emergency blanket. A solar battery, charger and waterproof case for the mobile phone.

Back to the scales and it weighed in at eighteen pounds. To keep within the self imposed limit, I can add only seven pounds of clothing.

We're walking in late August warmth, therefore I could swap the fleece - a heavy item - for a lightweight cotton jumper. Then, according to my inventory I was taking a waterproof jacket and a poncho to cover me and the backpack. Thinking pragmatically I could forgo the poncho and just use the rain cover that came with the back pack. Add in two pairs of walking trousers, one for evening wear and the other tough and waterproof for daily use. Two extra running shirts.

Three pairs of socks, I'd bought ankle-length already to save weight. Underwear, sleepwear and I almost forgot the tick remover. Hmm. Let's hope we don't have to use that. That all weighed twenty-five pounds and *a bit*. I told myself not to worry about *the bit*.

Except that when it came to the day of departure, despite the fact that I knew my weight limit had already been reached I realised that I had failed to pack a ten pack of tissues, sun tan lotion (ha-ha-ha), insect repellent and a guidebook with a pen. There's a part of me that didn't want to know the damage but I was inexorably drawn to the bathroom scales only to discover I was three pounds over the limit. My reflection in the bathroom mirror had a quizzical look. What can be done? Should I abandon all my clothes and walk in what I am wearing? Never mind. It will just have to be carried. Anyway it was only 12.7 kilos which sounded much lighter already.

**Chris:** As leaving day drew close, I started loading up and weighing the rucksack and was pleasantly surprised to find that my stuff was pretty much within limits. Essentially clothing included two of everything required for walking, that is trousers, shirts and socks so that in theory I could always have one to change into. A thin, lightweight but warm top for walking on colder days found its way in there along with a thicker fleece which would be sported on evening trips to the pub. I also bought a very light pair of shoes for evening wear, to allow some relief from the boots. Thanks again to modern materials and fabrics the total weight of the clothing was acceptable, leaving space for other bits of essential equipment like a torch, spare specs, toilet roll, phone charger, first aid kit, some ibuprofen, the solar panel and sun cream - that weather related optimism again! Even with the tent and sleeping bag stowed in the bottom pocket, the rucksack, at sixty-five litres wasn't actually filled by all this stuff, but I resisted the temptation to fill up the spare capacity, knowing that we'd need a bit of space to accommodate daily food supplies we'd buy along the Way.

When departure day arrived, I felt well prepared for what we were about to do, both in terms of how we were equipped and also physically. Always tending towards overweight, I was currently tipping the scales at only slightly more than my target weight of thirteen and a half stones, the lightest I'd been since we'd completed the Way the first time. We both lost weight the first time and I was expecting to do so again, but I was comfortable with where I was for now.

**Duncan:** I checked my kit for the very last time then slipped the water bottles into the outer pockets of the sack, shoved my walking boots into a bag and laid the backpack in the boot of my car. It seemed to fill the entire space.

We drove to Chris's house in Saffron Walden where Mag had laid on some coffee and home baking while we discussed the health and happiness of various members of our families, the most concerning of whom was Mag's mother, who'd been a resident of a nursing home for some time.

**Chris:** In early August I'd found that by coincidence our friends Andy and Barbara were heading off for a break in the Lake District on the same day that we planned to leave for Edale. Barbara had very kindly offered to take us there, it being sort of on the way. Before accepting gratefully I'd pointed out that we'd each have a big pack but she was happy we'd fit into the car ok. Mag was grateful too as it meant she wouldn't get lumbered for driving to Derbyshire and back.

Our chauffeurs arrived just after eleven and we couldn't help but notice that they were in a Ford Focus, rather than one of the larger vehicles they owned and that I'd expected. Duncan and I exchanged concerned glances as we wondered how four adults and their holiday gear were going to fit in this car at all, let alone enjoy a comfortable journey. Somehow though, we got it all in, our packs in the boot and much of their luggage in the cab and stuffed in every nook or cranny that could be found. We said our emotional goodbyes to Sylvie and Mag. Duncan chose not to put a date on our return when I optimistically (foolishly?) told Mag I'd see her in seventeen days.

Andy is an old friend of us both, yet another alumnus of the

## We'll never get that in the boot

photography course. We'd had only occasional contact in the immediate post student years but in the late 80's he and Barbara had moved to Saffron Walden, a short time before Mag and I settled there. We became much closer after that, Mag and Barbara got on well and our children were good buddies as they grew up together.

**Duncan:** Andy was one of the more gregarious students during college days. He stood out because he stayed in a scout hostel near Stepney and his whole life seemed to revolve around the morals and rules of the scout movement. Andy resembled in outlook the Blue Peter presenter John Noakes (he would have been a physical double if John Noakes had been a bit broader of beam and hailed from the Essex marshes), with a remarkable have a go attitude that influenced everything he did.

Andy had walked a major part of the Pennine Way as a young lad in a company of scouts. It sounded like he had quite an ordeal, more of an endurance march than an adventure. The Way had only been open for a few years and route finding was still a matter of dispute. Also the walkers crossing the moors and bogs were beginning the pattern of erosion that would lead to significant interventions later. It was not a golden memory for Andy but like all who have walked the Pennine Way, the fascination remains.

The questions came thick and fast on the journey up. Do we have a tent? We both have tents, lightweight jobs. The water bottles; they have special technology to filter out nasty microbes, because water is the heaviest item to carry, so filling up as we go along can keep the weight down. Will we do it? Well, we hope so but you never know with the Pennine Way.

**Chris:** The drive took us north on the A1 before we turned on to the A57 near Worksop. An echo of the past, but this time there was no childhood home or family to drop in on. The 1979 road would have taken us past the streets where I grew up, but there was no opportunity to bore my fellow travellers with nostalgia as the newer ring road circumnavigated the town and steered us toward Sheffield and the Peak District beyond.

Discussion of every aspect of walking the Pennine Way continued, particularly our, and Andy's, remembrance of all those years ago. Andy apparently still has a tangible reminder of his experience as a fourteen year old on the Way. Close to the path, he can't remember exactly where, he found a fossil and popped it in his day sack, took it home and to this day the relic resides at his father's house. Knowing Andy as we do, it seems entirely in character when he told us that this 'fossil' weighed in at thirty-two pounds! Enough to blow a hole in the most ambitious walker's max. pack weight strategy.

As we headed west, the sky grew darker and rain began to fall, lightly at first but becoming heavy and persistent. None of us were encouraged by this, Andy and Barbara spotting that coming from the west as it was, the weather was probably doing similar work in the Lakes.

Arriving in Edale by mid afternoon, we parked outside the Old Nags Head. Sited just yards away from the first Pennine Way sign, the pub proudly proclaims itself the 'official start'. It's also just across the road from the campsite, so under a temporarily dry but still threatening sky, we unpacked and said our thank yous and goodbyes to our generous chauffeurs.

I'd had an idea that once we'd established base camp we'd go for a late afternoon stroll to Hollin's Cross on the ridge between Edale and Castleton, and maybe even take a look at Mam Tor, but somehow the conditions weren't conducive. A hazy plan made for a sunny day.

## *Chapter Three*

**Duncan:** We knocked on the scuffed black door of Cooper's Campsite. While we stood in the spitting rain the owner cautiously opened the door just enough for the smell of stale cigarette smoke to edge out of the office. He was probably about our age although he looked a lot older in his stained denim dungarees. He told us that the campsite is in the field behind some farm buildings and tents are pitched on the left.

On the way to the field we passed the cafe. It was closed now but the owner had said that it opened for breakfast at 9.00 am each morning, which we thought a bit late in the day, as we were hoping to be on the move by then. Around the corner we took a detour to look inside the toilet block. The toilet stalls resembled those found in the school playgrounds of my youth and the showers needed twenty pence pieces to work. The overall ambience was of a concrete cowshed and it was obvious that the 'glamping' revolution had yet to be felt in Edale.

Back outside the rain petered out so we walked up the field through long wet grass and in a gusting wind to find a suitable pitch. Overall the temperature was a few degrees below desirable but at least there was merely moisture in the air rather than raindrops. We dropped our gear in a sheltered spot by a drystone wall.

I have practiced putting up the tent twice. On the second occasion I slept in it overnight to make sure I was happy with all the kit. During that day we had walked fifteen miles on the hottest day on record in the UK. The mercury hit 38.7° C at the Cambridge Botanical Garden a few miles north west of where we walked. Later on that evening I erected the tent in the garden, thinking it would be a cooler place to sleep. Sylvie was rather puzzled by my wish to sleep outdoors when there was a perfectly serviceable indoor option available. Retiring to my tent in the darkness I found a wasp had made itself at home and using my headlight and some cardboard I wrangled it out into the night. The lesson learnt was to keep the flap closed unless I wanted to share the night with vagabond insects.

That night I slept fitfully, woken by gusting winds, the approaching rumble of thunder and flash of lightning, followed by a torrent of rain. The tent remained dry and it was definitely a lot cooler than sleeping in the house. Once the dawn broke I slunk inside to enjoy a few hours in my own bed. It was my birthday, after all.

Practice does not make perfect and it took half an hour to sort out my tent and the various items inside. The long grass softened the ground and my previous sleeping experience gave the interior a familiar feel. The temperature though was not familiar as there was a definite autumnal chill and I was glad I'd decided to buy a two season sleeping bag, despite the extra weight.

**Base camp, Edale**

Having set our camp it was now four o'clock and time to get social. I'd bought a new camera with an app which allowed me to control it using my mobile phone. I clumsily took a picture of Chris's foot, then two of me looking down the lens, before setting the camera on a drystone wall to take a group photo. Next I managed to record a video of the two of us looking down at the app and up at the camera. I finally succeeded to capture a photograph on the fourth attempt. In theory I was supposed to be able to preview the pictures on my phone and select one to WhatsApp the folks back home. It turned out there was not a chance of me achieving this feat without resorting to the two hundred and forty page online manual. So I slipped out my mobile phone and took a selfie. Not the best start for two allegedly professional photographers.

*Chapter Three*

## Two allegedly professional photographers

This selfie wasn't easy either, especially trying to get some campsite ambience into the frame but with communication achieved, we headed off for a wander around the village. The rain having relented, we passed many a dishevelled hiker leaving a watery trail as they returned to their evening accommodation after a long day up on the peaks.

Down by the railway station there's a second cafe and that's the sum total of Edale's facilities, so we headed back to the nearest pub, the Rambler Inn. Here they offered b&b accommodation and although the bed part was of no interest to us, if they could be persuaded to provide us with breakfast at an earlier hour, that would be. Having ordered our pints we asked to speak to the manager and put this proposal to him. He firmly re-buffed us with a look that suggested that this was one of the most offensive requests he had ever heard. A disappointment, as we thought this was a cunning plan. We were baffled as to why any business that was already providing a service wouldn't want to make a bit more money. Never mind, nine o'clock at Cooper's Campsite it will have to be, we might have to start later than we expected but at least we will be fed.

Unimpressed by the welcome in the Ramblers Inn, we headed back to the Old Nags Head and ordered dinner. We were both aware of the dangers of overindulgence on the first night. Our failed attempt to walk the White Peak Way back in the early eighties started at Bakewell where the nearest pub had negotiated an extension to midnight. Heaven knows why at six o'clock when we crossed the threshold we thought that would be of interest to us but we drank steadily until this new closing time and for steadily, you should really read excessively.

## *Chapter Three*

After the final bell at ten past midnight we were left with a long walk back along the A6 to the campsite, during which I decided it was a good idea to follow the double white lines in the centre of the bending road while singing the chorus from the Dr Hook song, 'Everyone's making it big but me'. Fortunately the A6 was blissfully free of traffic at 00.30 on a Sunday morning so I avoided a trip in an ambulance.

We were in quite a state that evening and the next day was pitiful. We barely walked six miles and I am sure we looked like escapees from a lunatic asylum.

In the Old Nags Head we had a pint with the meal and a whisky to warm us on our way. This was almost abstemious. As we sipped the Talisker, Chris began to talk seriously about the plans of his eldest daughter. She is about to buy a house with her boyfriend in Canada and they will move there later in the year, once they have both found jobs nearby. Then there will be a wedding and it is hoped sometime after that the patter of tiny feet and I feel a numbing melancholy for my friend, the idea of grandchildren across the other side of the pond. Chris carried on with what I suspected was a speech that he had practiced before we left, because his daughter has a plan. A plan to relocate not just Chris and Mag but her brother and sister as well and plant them in what she perceives to be the more fertile ground of Canada, with jobs and homes and a picture perfect future of the next generation. As Chris related these details, the numbing melancholy that I had felt earlier for my friend of over forty-five years was transferred to me.

In the darkness we made our way back to the tents and wished each other goodnight. I slipped into my night clothes and lay awake contemplating the future that Chris had outlined. As yet another aircraft from Manchester airport ascended slowly over the campsite I put the thoughts to one side. There was really nothing for me to do but be supportive.

The clouds melted away to reveal a starry darkness. It was becoming obvious that my tent was an unnecessarily long distance from the toilets. There was a judgement to be made here as to be too close risks a night broken by an endless shuffle of urgent campers. However my lengthy journey to the toilet block was now a matter for regret.

*Chapter Three*

Especially since the plummeting temperature seemed to be matched by a similar decrease in my bladder capacity which led to several trips across the long wet grass, alive with the red eyes of wary rabbits.

**The clouds melted away…**

# FLASHBACK

**August 18, 1979**

In woollen trousers, garishly checked shirts and twenty-five pound rucksacks on our backs, we met at King's Cross Station and took the train to Retford. On arrival we were collected from the station by Chris's father in his brown Vauxhall Nova. He drove us to Worksop and that afternoon we walked to Clumber Park. Like cramming just before an exam, we wanted to make sure our legs were still working before the real challenge.

Back at the house as the sun set on a warm evening we took a trip around the immaculately kept garden, ending with his father's pride and joy, the greenhouse. Inside there were strongly fragranced ruby red tomatoes which were both a treasure and a memento, tomatoes whose flavour far outshone those from a greengrocer's stall but the taste was bittersweet as for him they rekindled memories of Italy during the war.

In the evening we went to a pub where Chris had arranged to meet up with some old friends from school. I talked for ages with the younger sister of one of his friends. A smart, sassy and fun brown-haired, brown-eyed girl who was studying at Leeds. For a magical hour I was caught in her spell and I wondered if I should postpone the Pennine Way, or maybe give it all up, leave London and move to Leeds.

It was that kind of evening.

We walked home, stopping for a fish and chip supper with mushy peas before turning in for the night to dream of what might have been.

**Opposite: that's the cleanest we'll be for the next sixteen days**

You can follow the route by using the QR code or this webpage link: https://www.wikiloc.com/hiking-trails/pw-1-edale-to-longdendale-40643582

**Pennine Way - take two**

2102 ft

Kinder Plateau

Snake Pass

Bleaklow

Longdendale

# Chapter 4 - Edale to Longdendale

746 ft

16.04 mi

Total ascent: 2018 ft

Total distance: 16.04 miles

August 29th

**Chris:** Just before 10am on 29th August 2019, Duncan and I found ourselves at the very place where forty years ago, my mum and dad had taken photographs of us, before proudly watching us turn and head off on 'that Pennine Way' as my dad usually called it. This time it was just the two of us. Nobody watched us positioning our cameras on the wall opposite the first Pennine Way sign, before hurriedly adopting the same positions we had back then. Neither were there witnesses to our ridiculous attempts to take smartphone selfies, as we struggled to get both of us and the signpost in the same picture. Where are your parents when you need them?

We stepped out of the lovely morning sunshine and into the cool of the woods on the first few yards of the Pennine Way. We were actually about to start, some fifteen months after we'd first decided we would reprise our finest hour. In an uncharacteristically sentimental moment, I wished Duncan luck for the walk and at the risk of making him ill, thanked him for having been my friend these forty years. Anyone walking behind us may have thought nothing of it, but they might even have seen me place my hand on Duncan's shoulder as these moving words tumbled out.

Out of the woods and on to the path heading towards Kinder Scout, it took less than a minute for me, for some reason already (needlessly) checking the route on my phone, to trip and go rucksack over elbow on to the hard stony track. The phone went flying off into the grass at the side of the path as my 'anti-gravity' pack proved anything but. Despite the fairly calamitous fall I was up in a moment, laughing off

**The first major problem, the trip hazard**

my clumsiness and reassuring Duncan that the grazed hand was nothing as we headed up Grindsbrook Clough. We medical people call this type of injury 'phone-related ambulatory trauma' (PRAT).

Grindsbrook Clough was the main route to Kinder Scout back in 1979, and what is now the main route, looping to the south of the plateau via Jacob's Ladder was an alternative. The reverse is true now, but Duncan had made a case for starting out as we had the first time. Having walked up Jacob's Ladder on a school trip and remembering how steep it is, I happily concurred. The first part of the climb to Kinder was delightful. The early sunshine had given way by now to a somewhat gloomy though unthreatening sky, but it was reasonably warm. We were sheltered in the Clough as we set a good pace along the low gradient, heather-bordered path. We took time to look behind us at the excellent scenery, back across the Vale of Edale towards the hills that separated it from the Hope Valley, where many years ago our attempt at the White Peak Way had faltered. We pressed on up, and it finally felt that we were on the Pennine Way.

Fairly soon the easy walk became steeper and then pretty much a scramble over huge rocks, often in the brook itself. For the first time, but far from the last it as it would turn out, it occurred to me that I didn't remember it being like this, as our pace dropped and we made slow progress along the steep and very rugged path. Hill walking at last! We would now find out if the months of preparation had been sufficient. It was worrying therefore when Duncan said he needed to take a rest for a few minutes, and in a concerned way told me that his legs felt like jelly. I was feeling ok: I can't say I wasn't finding it tough going but reasoned that the top wasn't really very far away.

**Grindsbrook Clough in 1979 - it's easily forgotten**

While we took a breather, I reflected on how we were doing so far and thinking I'd wet my whistle I discovered I'd already lost my water bottle. I imagine it had dislodged from the pack when I fell over. I had a spare fortunately, but the loss added to the feeling that things were not going perfectly. We were some way behind schedule: not that we had a precise plan of where we should be at what time, but we knew from experience that Day 1 was a long and tough one, and getting off to a good start would be key to ending the day well.

# Chapter Four

A walk of two halves, the day consists of conquering Kinder before descending to the Snake Pass, where the second half, the task of crossing Bleaklow begins. On our first two visits we'd found route finding across the featureless black terrain of Bleaklow very difficult and the walking over the wet, sludgy peat very demanding. Each time we'd descended from the moor at a different point, nowhere near the actual path, or indeed, the day's ultimate destination, the youth hostel at Crowden.

This time the day had started early, more because we had both had a dreadful night's sleep in our newly purchased, hi-tech, super lightweight tents, rather than that we were keen to get ahead. After my first night in a tent for thirty-five years I felt a bit spaced out, just like I'd felt on numerous occasions recently after sleepless nights in A&E with Mag and her mum - whose failing health was necessitating periodic emergency admission - but much, much colder. Gritty eyed and worrying that our plan to camp most nights had been at the very least naïve, we'd slowly repacked our rucksacks while waiting for the campsite's café to open. Warmed by a bit of activity, I had taken in the surroundings with apprehension, excitement and an odd sense of detachment from real life. The sight of Grindslow Knoll rising up against a clear sky, had given me hope for a good day.

A good day always starts with a good breakfast of course, so just before nine we'd headed to the campsite's café, only to find that it was closed on Thursdays. It being Thursday, we found this rather disappointing, especially as yesterday the old boy had assured us that we'd be able to get breakfast at nine o'clock. To be fair, he hadn't said which day. As a result we'd found ourselves walking in exactly the wrong direction, heading to the Penny Pot café at the southern end of the village.

Not the prompt start we'd hoped for. Then, having broken our fast and heading toward the starting post, I'd suddenly been overtaken by severe abdominal pain, requiring a quick return to the campsite's facilities. A further twenty minute delay until I'd got it out of my system, as it were. No reflection on the Penny Pot I'm sure, though perhaps the previous night's chilli hadn't been the wisest choice. Or was it just apprehension, anxiety for what lay ahead?

Back up in Grindsbrook, we were by now feeling refreshed and ready to go again so we resumed the ascent. The path continued in much the same vein, before suddenly levelling off and depositing us on the edge of Kinder, where straight away I recognised the other-worldly rock formations that pepper the plateau. One such looked especially familiar; I'd photographed it the first time and could clearly remember printing the picture all those years back when that meant enlargers and sploshing about in developer and fix.

The view today was not particularly welcoming as off to the west we could see banks of dark cloud heading towards us. First time round we'd been exceptionally lucky meteorologically speaking, there having

**The other-worldly formations that pepper the plateau (and overleaf)**

**Wool Packs**

**The more obvious path**

been only a couple of days when we'd had any serious rain. The weather forecasts for the early part of September this time showed a clear north south divide: the south - home - would be pleasant and warm in an autumnal way, but the north was expected to be subject to strong westerly winds and a lot of rain. There was clear evidence that the forecast might be accurate at least as far as today was concerned as rain started to fall, and a strengthening wind kept us colder than we'd ideally like to be.

I'd expected that route finding on top of Kinder would be easier than we'd found it before when both times we had struggled to work out where we were supposed to be heading. I expected the paths to be more obvious now, and indeed there are many paths criss-crossing the area, but for a time we were unsure which way we should be going. Taking a general 'head west' strategy we eventually hit the edge of the plateau and for the first time joined the 'official' route a little way north of Jacob's Ladder.

The path was very obvious now and we were at last able to push on at a good pace, soon arriving at Kinder Downfall. We'd seen a good number of walkers out on the plateau but here all of a sudden there were crowds of people all settling down for lunch at the popular vantage point. We continued past them, with views down the steep side of the hill to the Kinder Reservoir and the village of Hayfield. Way beyond, through the increasingly dense grey, was a suggestion of the Manchester metropolis.

As we approached the northern edge of Kinder, over a drink and early afternoon snack we agreed that we were behind where we ought to be, and admitted to a concern that it could be quite late by the time we were finding our way off Bleaklow. We were pleased that now the path started to head generally downwards and we could keep up the good pace, though the rocky nature of the path meant that concentration was needed to avoid turning an ankle.

The path dropped down from the northern limits of Kinder to the relatively low lying land between Kinder and Bleaklow and headed across nearly three miles of very wet terrain. Here for the first time we really appreciated the miracle of the paved path. The route toward

**Looking back to Kinder plateau from the Snake Pass path**

Featherbed Moss and the Snake Pass was a continuous parade of massive flagstones raised just a couple of centimetres above what would otherwise have been a very uncomfortable walk indeed. We marvelled at the scale of the mission to get the flagstones here, but were very glad that someone had chosen to accept it.

There being no real hills in Essex, we had challenged ourselves during preparation with distance and speed, often hitting an average of nearly four miles an hour even with (almost) full packs over eighteen to twenty miles in a day. Here then, on this excellent surface, we were well equipped to really crack on and when we arrived at Doctor's Gate on the Snake Pass we were, for the first time, comfortable with our overall progress. Additionally, we'd come out from under the cloud that was sitting on Kinder and were now enjoying a bright, sunny afternoon as we left behind the A57 traffic noise and headed towards Bleaklow.

After the miracle of the flagstones of Featherbed Moss came the revelation of Bleaklow. Forty years ago we'd laboured across a black expanse of peat hags, sliding down into the wet bottoms and clambering back up the other side of gullies often deeper than we were tall. It was physically challenging, and made route finding almost impossible. Now though, thanks to the amazing regeneration work that has taken place on the moor since our first visit, we found instead a beautiful place. Far from the trial we'd anticipated, the completion of day one would be straightforward, hugely enjoyable and painless. We progressed without difficulty, our legs brushed by the heather that grew profusely at either side of the firm path, heading initially north and then turning west toward Crowden.

The paths of Bleaklow were less populated than those of Kinder but here we did encounter a number of youngsters engaged on their Duke of Edinburgh's award challenge. They seemed somewhat weary, and one particular young lad, progressing slowly on crutches didn't appear to be having a great time, but they responded reasonably brightly to our helloes. While the Duke's award scheme may be character building and inspire in some a lifetime's love of the outdoor life, I can't help thinking that many are probably put off walking forever.

**Bleaklow Head, with Duke of Edinburgh walkers**

A little later we met an older gent, out on the moor for the day having taken the train down from York. He made me think how much I want to carry on walking such places at his age and beyond. Perhaps it's the way he likes it, but it seemed slightly sad that he was alone: with luck Duncan and I will be able to continue our joint outings for many years to come.

Feeling buoyed by the pleasant afternoon sunshine that we'd been enjoying since emerging from the cloud that hugged Kinder, and with confidence bolstered by the unexpectedly agreeable terrain it came as a real blow to suddenly be hit by a sharp pain in my right knee. Possibly an effect of the earlier impact, but this was more like discomfort I'd felt before. I was afraid that my worst fear was being realised as with every step I was reminded that I had previously been diagnosed with a damaged meniscus in the knee. Although it had settled down and been problem free for some time, I despaired that it should choose now, Day 1, to recur.

Some years ago, one of our May walking trips had taken us to Slovakia where a week of fairly tough walking had been made more challenging by wet, cold weather and some very steep, muddy slopes. I was left with a troubling lack of mobility in my left knee which worsened in the following months to the extent that I eventually sought medical opinion. An MRI scan showed some serious localised damage to an area of cartilage and surgery was judged to be necessary, to clean up the damaged meniscus and remove the floating bits of debris inside the joint that could cause problems in the future.

Following a successful procedure I was walking freely again by the next May, only to fall prey to the same symptoms in my right knee a few months later. The same surgeon diagnosed the same problem and prescribed the same solution. This time though the knee seemed to right itself while I waited for a surgery date, and so when it turned out that the referral letter for my surgery had been lost and I wasn't on a waiting list anyway, I decided not to pursue it. Subsequently I'd had three years of trouble free walking, until today.

Weirdly, steps up or especially down shallow gradients invoked the sharpest pain and I soon learned to lead with the left foot as we now turned north west to start the descent to Longdendale. The path was good with heavy vegetation at either side and we were soon enjoying a fine view down the steep sided Torside Clough to the reservoir beyond. Not very much further to go before I could rest up and allow the knee (hopefully) to recover, but at the back of my mind – the idea remained unspoken for now – was the thought that if it didn't recover our second attempt might be over pretty well before it had begun.

Day 1's (and tomorrow night's) accommodation was to be in the relative comfort of a b&b: I'd figured that after the first day a night in the tent would not be welcome and so had booked this quite some time before. The Old House is perfectly placed, hardly five hundred metres off the path, so we arrived there minutes after the final brief but fairly steep descent from the Bleaklow section of the walk. We were greeted by the proprietor Joanne and invited into the dining room for a welcome cuppa. I was pleased to de-boot and take the weight off my knee, and enjoy some relief from the pain which worryingly, I had not been able to walk off.

Despite that it was a good feeling to have completed the first day and we were able to compare notes with a husband and wife team, Simon and Wendy, who arrived at much the same time as us. Joanne and the man of the house, James regaled us with Pennine Way tales and meetings with other noteworthy walkers as we chatted into the late afternoon. With James the hind legs of no donkey were safe and his stories, punctuated every five or six words by 'yer know wha' a mean don't yer' were highly entertaining, featuring a range of subject matter from the exploits of dangerously unprepared walkers to the local farmer who was making a killing producing 'honey from Upper Thong', a nearby village.

The Old House offers not only b&b but provides transport to and from the start and end points of the first few days' walking. James, raconteur and as it turned out driver, was booked to collect us from Standedge at the end of Day 2 and return us there on the morning of Day 3. Evening transport to the local pub is also provided by James, so after a leisurely couple of hours in which we washed bits of clothing, showered, had a snooze and I dosed up on ibuprofen, we met James on the drive to be chauffeured to the nearby village of Padfield. By now we were feeling pretty tired but relaxed, and we enjoyed a couple of pints and a good pub meal served up at the Peels Arms.

Also dining was the old gent we'd met earlier on Bleaklow. Interestingly, he turned out to be one of the few walkers we've ever encountered who have experienced the Offa's Dyke long distance path. One of our less glorious outings had seen us endure two and a half days of solid rain before we gave up the Welsh border path, bedraggled and miserable, somewhere near Wrexham. Our drinking partner's experience had been better, suggesting that we'd maybe just been unlucky. Perhaps my belief that it always rains in Wales is misguided and that one day we should have another go at that one too. Something to discuss with Duncan over the many miles head, if indeed there were to be many miles ahead. The pain in my knee had eased, though I remained anxious that the problem could be terminal in terms of completing this walk.

Duncan and I took it in turns to go outside and phone home. Sylvie and Mag had both been very understanding in going along with our plan to revisit this walk. I had certainly never been apart from Mag for such a long period of time and although over the years Duncan's work had taken him away from home for days at a time, three weeks away from Sylvie was also unprecedented. At least mobile technology made it easy to keep in contact.

The first part of the conversation was to find out the status of Mag's mum, who'd been unwell for the previous few days. Suffering chronic renal failure, for some time Brenda's health had followed a cyclical pattern of periodic hospitalisation followed by spells of seemingly better health. The hospitalisations were becoming more frequent, but she always seemed to pull out of the trough and keep going. Though bed-bound and losing her short term memory, she remained cheerful

and was always overjoyed to see Mag who visited every day. Over the years we had been repeatedly amazed by the resilience Brenda had shown, but we both felt that this dip seemed more serious. We wondered whether she'd have the strength or even the desire to pull out of this one. Mag reported that there hadn't been much change, but that a different antibiotic had been prescribed and there was hope that its effect might kick in soon.

Chauffeur James' schedule involved picking up residents from the pub at 9.30pm – if you wanted to stay later you were on your own. I'd looked into the possibility of getting a taxi back later but in truth by the deadline we were ready to go back. Tiredness was definitely kicking in. Very glad that we weren't camping again, we returned to Old House and the warmth and comfort of our twin beds where we both nodded off in front of the 10 o'clock news.

**Look upon my peat hags and despair. Bleaklow, '79**

# FLASHBACK

**August 19, 1979**

Whatever we might have felt about the Pennine Way, the weather gave a grey shrug of disinterest as we walked up Grindsbrook Clough to Kinder plateau. The path was not new to us as we had walked this way back in Easter but the terrain was very different. Back then the cold and snow had firmed the ground and filled the peat groughs.

Here was peat in the raw and it meant business.

On the slopes of Bleaklow the peat-scape became eternal, a wallow, a land without landmarks, where the imprints of passing walkers were quickly swallowed. The guidebook and compass were our only friends.

**Chris clutches his trusty Wainwright while crossing Bleaklow**

Mapping:
https://www.wikiloc.com/hiking-trails/pw-2-longdendale-to-standedge-40723469

Laddow Rocks

# Chapter 5 - Longdendale to Standedge

Total ascent: 4229 ft | Total distance: 28.84 miles

August 30th

The tardy cock

**Duncan:** I was woken by the cock's crow despite having had a broken night's sleep. This cock was not an early riser, it being some considerable time after dawn and maybe due to its tardy start it'd decided that once was enough as any more noise would just draw attention to its lack of punctuality. As I lay awake I wondered about the state of my body after the first day and to my astonishment I found that my legs and feet felt good and even my back was not complaining. This new backpack was proving to be even more comfortable than I could have hoped (these are not words I ever thought I would write).

The night before I'd washed some clothes so I headed to the drying room to check them over. Although clean, they were still damp but since we were returning that evening they could dry off during the day. This was not a good sign for the rest of the journey because if clothes won't dry overnight in ideal conditions then how would they fare in the tent? Time will tell.

In the dining room Wendy and Simon who we'd met the day before were already up and eating bacon and eggs. Outside a group of Duke of Edinburgh walkers had camped on the grass and were now packing their tents, then shouldering their packs before reluctantly trudging off towards the woods. Once they'd disappeared their teachers (or assessors, as they preferred to style themselves) came inside for breakfast. We ordered a packed lunch and prepared to leave as around us there was a discussion between James and the teachers about the latest Brexit shenanigans.

Back in the room Chris fished out a lightweight backpack, a flimsy piece of nylon from what I could see, in which he intended to carry his essentials for the day. Meanwhile I removed the items I didn't want to lug around from my pack.

We left just after nine o'clock. Yesterday's wind was still howling and the weather was overcast as we followed the muddy tracks of the Duke of Edinburgh walkers across the field and down to the woods. My new boots were slipping around alarmingly in the mud.

A month earlier, during one of our Thursday practice walks we had our first major wet weather challenge. It rained with vigour and at the same time the path turned to cross a field shoulder high with broad bean plants. For a quarter of a mile it was as if we were being targeted by a crack team of Essex firefighters armed with buckets of water and a strong desire to halt our progress. My puny gaiters offered no protection from this onslaught and my trousers and boots were thoroughly soaked.

When I got back home and inspected my footwear there seemed to be some cracks in the leather and I wondered if they were no longer waterproof. I resorted to my other pair of boots and for the next two weeks I wore them but there was a reason why I didn't favour this pair. Although initially a good fit, by the end of a full day's walking my feet had swollen up and were badly cramped. I didn't think I could take this punishment for the whole Pennine Way, so reluctantly Sylvie and I went shopping once more.

In the store I tried on a make of boot that I knew was suitable for my large, broad feet and they were perfectly comfortable. For a quarter of an hour I rambled purposefully around the shop attempting to look like an experienced hiker. Then the assistant suggested that for feet like mine (broad Germanic feet apparently), there was another brand that I had never tried before. To my surprise they were immediately much more comfortable than the boots I knew and trusted. Added to this they were very lightweight, almost half the weight of my previous boot.

As Frances Morris, the director of the Tate Gallery said when interviewed on Desert Island Discs, 'You can walk further in comfortable shoes' and this is just the type of practical advice I needed at this time. (I may revisit this quote at some later point along the walk.) Flushed with success we went on to buy a pair of waterproof walking trousers which alongside my backpack turned out to be the best buy of the lot.

We reached the starting point for the day and almost immediately had to make our way through a phalanx of parked white vans that had deposited a group of unenthusiastic gardeners. They were disconsolately pushing pruned branches around the stoney path with their brooms. As we approached the Torside reservoir there were more gardeners at work. One of whom, impervious to the effect of gravity was driving a lawnmower up the steep grassy face of the reservoir.

**The starting point for the day**

In the distance could be heard the rumble of the main Manchester to Sheffield road, seemingly one long stream of heavy goods vehicles. When we

**Impervious to the effect of gravity**

arrived at its edge a gap magically appeared in this continuous train of traffic and we scurried across. Beyond we followed a farm track that climbed above the main road and from this vantage point we looked back at Bleaklow. Happy that yesterday's walk over the Kinder plateau had been much more enjoyable than we had anticipated, we turned north and so began the morning's work. A long climb to the top of Black Hill.

Underfoot the conditions were good, firm ground on a well defined route. After a mile or so we caught up with the first walker that we'd seen that day. He had strayed a hundred yards or so from the main path and seemed to be making slow progress toward a stream. As we passed him we came across a peculiar warning sign low on the path which he obviously had not spotted, that read 'Beware deep bog' and was referring very much to the direction he was headed. He glimpsed us and began to turn back. As we walked on I kept a careful eye on him until he made the safety of the path.

The path headed above Laddow Rocks and it started to feel strangely unfamiliar. It turned out that it did not always go this way as forty years ago it stayed below the rocks and carried on up the valley. We'd heard of some walkers who'd taken the old route recently and only managed to progress by walking on the top of the sunken posts of an old fence.

This high level route was much firmer and as the path reached the crest it held to the edge allowing an extensive view along the shallow valley. I wouldn't have given the height a second thought if it had not been for hearing about a man who had been walking from Land's End to John o'Groats and right here discovered that he suffered from vertigo, so he retreated and apparently threw in the towel.

I questioned when I stopped fearing heights. I remember that I used to become intensely nervous when close to an edge such as this. My imagination would picture me slipping and falling to my doom so every footstep would've caused me heightened anxiety. No longer though, I even have time to enjoy the view as long as I carefully watch my step.

Our walking holidays to Spain and beyond have taken us along

**The view from Laddow Rocks**

many a dazzling height. There was the Iparla crest in the Pyrenees. A long spectacular ridge, the Spanish side a shallow slope and on the other, a sheer cliff overlooking a French valley. Nearby we had walked the Peñas de Itxusi, two and a half miles of spectacular mountainside where the griffon vulture nests. Every fifty yards revealed another amazing vista as squadrons of these huge creatures took to thermals and glided serenely along the valley, the only noise being the flow of air over their finely feathered wings. On the final turn before joining La Grande Randonnée 10, one of the classic trans-Pyrenees routes, the path shrunk to a thin earthy strip just one step wide where one slip could lead to a catastrophic fall down a thousand feet of steep grassy slope.

Strangely, none of these walks had given me any concern but earlier this year we journeyed to the Vikos Gorge and for the first time in years I did feel the fear and retreated to the safety of the rock face while on some of the spectacular overlook paths. However it is rare

that I find myself on a path beside a sheer three thousand feet drop.

We followed the edge until Crowden Great Brook and the old path joined us. Here in years gone by the OS map was marked with the weasel words, 'Pennine Way undefined' indicating that, 'here be bog' and the route across was very much what you could make it. Now a precise line of flagstones meandered into the distance.

Ahead of us we could see Wendy and Simon in their matching Tilley hats and we soon caught up with them as they were crossing a stream. I asked Wendy if she needed any more pain relieving gel as her ankle was causing her problems yesterday. I had helped her out earlier by giving her some of mine when we saw them at breakfast. Wendy replied that her ankle seemed to be holding up.

We ploughed on leaving them in our wake. Ahead the grasses, sedges and reeds gave the hilltop a greenish brown hue and Black Hill it seemed, no longer lived up to its name.

**The meandering path to the trig point on Black Hill**

# FLASHBACK

**August 20, 1979**

It was a dank and dismal morning as we trudged up the path from Crowden. The greenery slowly gave way to a sea of peat which gradually dissolved into the boggy morass of Black Hill, a featureless mound with no discernible path. The leaden skies were lightening and the gentle drizzle came to an end.

At the trig point we stopped and looked around at the other walkers. Within a mile could be seen several pairs and groups of hikers walking the Way. A couple of lads in particular stood out as they squelched

past in jeans. Huge flapping flares of denim that wicked up the moisture and spread the dark peat up their legs.

Now I wonder of those two denim-clad walkers, did they look at us in our tweeds and think, 'what a pair of southern softy posers?' Probably, as there was little camaraderie on the Way in those days.

The sloppy mess of Black Hill

When we made our way across the top of Black Hill all those years ago, it appeared as the name implied that the exposed peat had been there forever. Little did we know that the landscape had been etched by acid rain from the coal fires of the industrial revolution. The Clean Air Act and the decline of heavy industry has brought the pollution to an end, and in the intervening years the National Park has worked tirelessly to reseed the barren moorland. Finally the flagstones have made the summit of Black Hill a very different place from the peat slop of yesteryear.

I believe that the flagstones on the Pennine Way should be regarded as one of the wonders of Britain. These old stones were hewn from the moors and laid as flooring for the heavy machinery in the cotton mills. They have borne the clatter of industry for over a hundred and fifty years. Then as the mills closed and were finally demolished, the

**Saved from the ever encroaching bog**

stone flooring was recovered and relaid near the places from which they were removed.

This is no city pavement though. These monumental stones have been laid face down directly on the moor and somehow they have not been swallowed by the bog. The surface is lumpy and jagged, with the added obstacle of the occasional old iron fastening that can trip the unwary, requiring constant vigilance.

Some people have questioned the use of flagstones and it's true that they are harder on the feet than walking on the spongy peat. I can only be grateful for the huge undertaking that has built this amazing trail in comparison to the horror of Black Hill all those years ago.

Since we climbed out of the valley the wind had been our constant companion, always at or around our faces and reaching the trig point offered an opportunity for some relief. However cowering close to the sheltered side we stumbled across several more young people doing their Duke of Edinburgh award. So far these were the only young people we had seen on the moors and I wondered if there were any youngsters who were walking without this coercion? Maybe this first experience of wild mountainside puts them off. After all the DofE is a challenge, requiring a specific number of miles in a set time and the inevitable consequence will be of tales told in warm classrooms of the sheer wretchedness of it all.

Black Hill is the highest point of today's walk and we were there in good time. It had been a steady morning and the afternoon promised to be a gentle downhill stroll.

On a previous occasion we took the old route across Dean Head Moss and then Featherbed Moss. A cosy and enticing name for one of the worst peat bogs on the old Pennine Way. However the route now headed in a more northerly direction, crossing Dean Clough, a deep valley cut into the peat, before reaching the A635 and all on well maintained flagstones. In less than an hour we arrived at the road where in a lay-by just a few yards further on there was the enticing possibility of coffee and sweets.

Dean Clough

Ahead of us was the bog-trotting walker we'd seen earlier. He'd picked up the pace and overtaken us and now gave the delights of the roadside café a miss. He then revised his decision and returned for refreshment. We were happy to stop and have a hot drink and an opportunity to converse with our fellow walker.

He told us he was from Ireland and was taking a few days off work to have a gander at this part of the Pennine Way. Like many lone walkers he was hesitant about engaging in conversation, that is for the evening, the common room of a youth hostel or the warm embrace of a pub. Or maybe he was going to wild camp which would allow him complete respite from any company. However, he can see that we're mostly harmless, especially when I mentioned that I was carefully watching his progress out of the bog earlier. He purchased a bacon roll along with his coffee and filled it with red sauce before hungrily dispatching it.

*Chapter Five*

The stall, sitting on an 'A' road in the middle of nowhere was being badly buffeted by the strong winds and I asked the middle aged lady who ran it if the weather was always this fierce. She was sure that this was unusual and handed us our hot coffees before starting to pack up. It was barely one o'clock and although the cafe was bathed in sunshine she had endured the battering from the wind for long enough. I helped her bring down the awning that covered the main hatch, fighting with a wind that was desperate to detain her. Wendy and Simon appeared from the moor and were her last customers of the day.

**One of the wonders of Britain**

**A curious sign**

We left our fellow walkers and carried on up a side road until we came to a curious sign. The artist Ashley Jackson began the 'Framing the Landscape' project on Wessenden Moor in the belief that the public needed to be reminded to take the time to look upon and reflect on what the land is, and how the geology, the weather, the wildlife and vegetation have acted to produce the scene. The importance of the standpoint and how this unique combination can affect or be affected by the observer. Much like astronomical physics you can begin to ask questions such as 'if I am not here to observe this, does it actually exist'. If this were a television programme it would be time to hand over to Professor Brian Cox and Dara O'Briain for a wise explanation.

I took against the whole project because of the quote under the frame. 'Many people look but only a few see'. Inferring a superiority of knowledge and experience merely from the act of viewing because we who stand here in the presence of the frame no longer 'look'. We apparently have achieved enlightenment and can now 'see'.

Hopefully not too many years will elapse before these frames are reduced to rust, their only reminder being a brown stain on the Yorkshire sod. At that moment the quote will have real meaning.

A mile or so further along, the path cut into the hillside and offered some respite from the wind. We sat down in this sheltered spot to have our packed lunches, contemplating the waves on Wessenden reservoir below. My packed lunch was so chilled it felt as though it has been taken directly out of a fridge and we realised that the weather, although dry, had been significantly colder than we'd anticipated.

As we walked down to Wessenden Lodge suddenly there was an unexpected choice of routes. Before we started Chris took it upon himself to make a route for each day using the Ordnance Survey map tool on his computer. He then sent me the GPS files and I converted them for the mobile phone application that I have used for years. Our experience was that these applications were both very good and the one that I use, Wikiloc, had two advantages over the OS map application. Firstly I can download an offline map so that it will always show where we are. Secondly it sounds an alert if we have strayed more than twenty yards from our planned path. This meant that when drafting a route we have to take a lot of care to follow even the smallest deviations. When we were out walking I used the Wikiloc app to follow the route and Chris referred to the OS map on his phone if there was ever any uncertainty.

Now the old hands out there will be muttering; paper and compass, technology can let you down. We used to think that as well. So here is what paper and compass does not tell you that tech can. We can know immediately where we are. We do not spend minutes scanning the horizon trying to work out if that church spire over there is this church and is that the road that goes here or could it be there. Fun though it is, almost everyone has mistaken a landmark and ended up straying from the path.

However the tech has to work and this is why we have both applications available. The mobile phone OS map application had one flaw and it was a pretty big one. It claimed to offer the possibility of downloading a route on to the phone but what it actually downloaded was the red line of our drawn route that we are following, not the map. This was served up over the mobile signal when we opened the application and therefore we needed to always have a good mobile signal. Otherwise we were standing looking at a blank screen with a red line snaking across it. Which was not useful, not useful at all. (To be fair they have made some significant changes to this app since we walked the Way.)

This was where the Wikiloc application came into its own because the map comes from Open Source maps which can be downloaded on to the phone, free, on a country by country basis, not merely the United Kingdom. Now these are not as detailed as the OS map, in that they will tell us where we are and where we are going but it won't tell us that we are surrounded by sinkholes for example. The main advantage is that with Wikiloc the map is always available, it does not need a mobile signal to work.

In use it works a bit like this. Occasionally the phone in my pocket will let out a little 'Weep, weep' noise and I will check the progress on the Wikiloc app. It will often have a red sign with the words 'You are leaving the route' and on checking the map I can see that the route has subtly changed over the years especially due to the flagstones which have been placed away from the old path to give an opportunity for regeneration. The map on the Wikiloc app will generally show that the path is in the right place but the route as planned from the old OS map is no longer correct. Carrying on the Wikiloc app will give a little cheery chime when we are back on the route. Most of the time we walk undisturbed.

A few weeks beforehand when I was buying some kit for the walk an ambitious sales person asked me how we were going to deal with route finding and I made the mistake of saying that we were going to rely on technology. This provoked a strong response along the lines of: the GPS sometimes does not work, especially in foggy conditions and what will we do then? I held back from suggesting that in a fog, let's face it, a map was not going to be a great help either and weaselled out by saying we had a back up map and compass. Which was half true as I did pack a compass.

However the other part of the technology which we do rely on is the GPS itself and in this regard some mobile phones are a lot better than others. Without wishing to name names, it does seem that the more expensive brands are inexplicably poor at GPS. I have a cheap Motorola phone and I rarely have any problem. It had a hard time following us as we walked down the Vikos Gorge but there were three thousand feet cliffs on either side.

Meanwhile, back at Wessenden Lodge there were several paths. The route that Chris had drawn followed the river before dipping into a valley and climbing out. However Wikiloc showed a different route also named the Pennine Way that crossed the face of the reservoir and contoured around to meet the drawn route. It was curious, the first of many anomalies that revealed that Wikiloc with its Open Source mapping, has another advantage. It is dynamic, in that in some situations the routes are more up to date, following the footsteps of real walkers rather than the right of way, as surveyed some time in the past.

A final point about mobile apps is that power is an essential requirement. The Wikiloc application was very light in its power use, the OS maps app in comparison burns through the mobile phone battery. We both had invested in solar panels with a

**Solar panels with power bank, sun optional**

power bank attached which since they weighed in at nearly a kilogram (not including the essential waterproof protection) was a significant part of the load. However we could not let a lack of power prevent progress.

I mention all this to show that we take route finding seriously as we have come to realise over several years of use that technology is not only completely transforming walking but it is also continually improving. Therefore to all those who still rely on the old ways I would now say that your misgivings are unfounded. It is glib to say that failure can happen because how often are people lost with a map and compass? If you were to ask me I would have to reply that most of the time I was using them I only had a hazy idea of my actual position.

We followed the route that Chris had drawn and as the track turned to the right another smaller path cut acutely left and down into the pretty green valley of Wessenden Brook, its sides threaded with purple heather. Crossing the brook we climbed steeply beside the burbling brown water of Blakely Clough and at the top we met the path that had contoured around and found ourselves skirting the northern edge of Black Moss. Looking north we could see two small reservoirs in front of us, the cold black water stirred to miniature white horses by the incessant wind. It was at this point that we were to ring our accommodation so that

**The pretty green valley of Wessenden Brook**

James could set off to meet us at Standedge.

It took us just over half an hour to get to the car park, where our Irish friend was poring over his maps. He was planning to walk on, probably to the White House Inn which would be another seven or eight miles. A day's journey that we made on the first occasion we walked the Way. He intended to finish his holiday when he reached Malham but we did not meet him again.

Although it was just after three o'clock we had decided before we started that it would be wise to shorten today's walk to allow for some recovery after crossing the Dark Peak. The walking however was not what we had expected and we could have easily carried on for a few more miles. James arrived and we bade farewell to our fellow traveller before driving back.

Along the way James liked to keep a running commentary. Although he's interested in us, he has probably heard all he needs to know about today's route and preferred to reel off his own litany of tales. Especially as we were passing near to Upper Thong and its honey, the tale retold with the inevitable 'Yer know wha' I mean don't yer'.

The drive back to the accommodation took nearly forty-five minutes as the roads skirted around the hills but finally we were back at the 'Old House' and happy to accept a coffee. A new group of walkers who'd come over from Edale that morning were also relaxing with a hot drink. Slowly we joined their conversation. They've made good time and we are impressed. We tell them about our day, and the fact that we have done the Way before and it turned out that only one of them, Rob, was walking the whole distance. His companions were here to cheer him on. His wife was going to be his support but due to a family illness she has to go back home and won't be able to return until practically the last day of the walk, across the Cheviot hills.

Rob started to talk of his itinerary because he had booked ahead, something he did very recently and he was apprehensive about one or two of the stages. There were places where all accommodation had already been booked, so he had to find alternatives, not all of them ideal. Since we were perceived to have some knowledge of the whole route Rob tentatively proffered a piece of paper with the places as booked.

He was intending to walk the Way in fourteen days and glancing at the sheet there was one day that stood out because it was not merely a long arduous walk but it also included the most elevation and some of the finest scenery. In our eyes this day would be very demanding but even more distressingly, would mean passing places where on a beautiful day it would be pleasant to linger and enjoy.

Of course the reality is that people are different and each of us is walking the Way to fulfil our own personal ambition. For me, it is an opportunity to rekindle memories and hopefully discover that I am not entirely wizened. What I wonder is it that motivates Rob?

After we had showered and changed, James was booked to take us back to the pub for dinner. On getting into the car he told us of the time that a couple of guests, who he suggested were 'ex-Army types' (yer know wha' I mean, don't yer) were staying overnight and wanted a lift to the pub. At the arranged time, James went to his car only to find one of the pair wandering aimlessly outside with a cup of tea, seemingly without a care in the world. James rather forthrightly told him the car was leaving right now whether he was ready or not and very quickly he shot back to his room and got changed. The next morning when he paid it was with a cheque from Coutts and the guest's name was heavily embellished with extra letters. James' curiosity was piqued and he discovered that he had hosted one of the commanders of the Falklands War. Because these walkers had booked the entire journey, James let the Pennine Way telegraph know of their impending visit. One of the owners further up the Way had asked the pair what they thought of James, to which they had diplomatically replied, 'he's to the point' which did rather sum him up.

Those who book in advance are probably unaware that their passage is watched and evaluated by the various staging posts along the Way. One group had been welcomed by enthusiastic barking as they entered the grounds and on opening the door their first comment to James was 'I hope you don't let dogs in here.' Reassured that the wildlife lived outside, they then spent the evening and the next morning grumbling and lamenting the food, the room, the temperature and all of the facilities. Indeed every single aspect of the stay was dissected and found wanting. The relief on seeing them leave was immense. When James delivered their bags to the next stop he warned the owners about the imminent arrival of the nitpicking guests, giving them the sobriquet 'the three witches'. The epithet stuck and for the next two weeks the arrival of the 'three witches' was a much feared and anticipated event and every place had its own story of extreme pernickertyness, which was gossiped along the bush telegraph.

Sitting in the cosy dining room of the Peels Arms in Padfield, we reminisced about how it was all those years ago. The first two days were a long flounder over a morass of peat. The names Kinder, Bleaklow and Black Hill were etched on my mind as places of unimaginable toil and struggle. I know that Chris has a long standing affection for this landscape but that was far from my opinion.The first

**A long flounder over a morass of peat**

time we came this way I had wondered to myself why the trespassers back in the 1930s on Kinder had made such a fuss about reclaiming this forsaken place. In all honesty I never wanted to see the Dark Peak again so when Chris first brought up the concept of coming back I had an unspoken reluctance about returning.

Now I have to admit that those trespassers have proven me wrong. The views across the Peaks were always dramatic but time, regeneration and most of all, the wondrous flagstones have transformed the thin trail.

*Chapter Five*

Later in the warmth of my bed, well fed, bathed and refreshed I reflected on just how smoothly it had gone so far. Lurking at the back of my mind was the nagging thought that we had better make the most of all this because from tomorrow it is time to start using our tents and living more frugally.

**The path to Snake Pass**

Mapping:
https://www.wikiloc.com/hiking-trails/pw-3-standedge-hebden-bridge-40723414

Nothing but blue skies

1598 ft

M 62 | White House public house | Stoodley Pike | Hebden Bridge

# Chapter 6 - Standedge to Hebden Bridge

800 ft 15.02 mi

Total ascent: 5092 ft Total distance: 43.86 miles

August 31st

**Chris:** Last night, outside the Peels Arms again, I had started my phone call with Mag using one of my typical opening conversational gambits: 'Hello beautiful gorgeous wife'. On this occasion my greeting was met by gales of laughter from not only Mag but a second female presence. I'd forgotten that Mag's friend Madeleine was visiting and staying overnight so they could do some serious catching up – they'd been flatmates in their late teens and early twenties but this was the first time they'd been together for twenty years. So that Madeleine could hear my voice, Mag had put the phone on speaker and it seemed that Madeleine was most impressed that after more than thirty years of marriage I was still addressing my wife in that way.

I was pleased that Madeleine was there keeping Mag company: although we were here with our wives' blessings there was in me a lingering feeling of something like guilt that we'd disappeared off for perhaps three weeks. As it turned out I'd have more reason to be grateful that Madeleine was in the house..

Day 3 began as Day 2 with the usual gradual effort to get organised and the short journey to the dining room for another excellent full English. Outside it was a bit grey and the weather forecasts suggested that today we'd probably have to put up with strong winds and rain. Packed and ready we braced ourselves for another verbal onslaught from James as we settled into the car for the journey back to where he'd picked us up the day before.

Relaxing in the back I switched on my phone for the first time that day. The phone of course has taken the place of the paper maps we had forty years ago, a technological advance undreamed of even just a few years ago. For our first trip, to save carrying all nine OS maps required, I had photocopied the necessary bits of the maps in the local library and then 'heat-sealed' the A4 pages back to back.

Unfortunately the only photocopying available at the time was in black and white so I also felt it necessary to colour the maps in – we had time on our hands back then. The resulting route map was divided up between us and the sheets slipped hardly noticed into our rucksacks.

**Packed and raring to go '79, the future laid out before us**

Now we had our phones which not only showed us the route, but also exactly where we were at all times.

We decided therefore that no paper maps were required this time, but realised we would be vulnerable if no charging facilities were available on days when we were camping. We hoped therefore that the solar cells we'd both invested in, which could be unfolded and strapped across the back of a rucksack, would solve any such problems. The combined weight of the cells and chargers was definitely greater than all the paper maps put together, but of course we depended on the phones for so much more than just routefinding.

The phone came to life and I was surprised by the familiar WhatsApp ting. I tapped on the single new message at the top of the list, from Mag: *Mum has died. I'm fine. You don't need to come back.* The care home had called in the early hours suggesting that Mag go there straight away, and she was with her mum as she peacefully slipped away a short time later.

For years we'd been anticipating this but now that it had actually happened I felt stunned, shocked and saddened. *You don't need to come back* – how could I not? The message had been left more than two hours earlier so I messaged Mag immediately thinking I'd call her as soon as I was out of the car. I broke the news to Duncan. I'm sure he had already considered the possibility of this happening, though we hadn't discussed it, and that he would probably expect that the walk would be over for me in this circumstance. Here I was though, saying I had Mag's instruction to carry on.

James very kindly offered to take us elsewhere or do whatever was necessary but first I called Mag from the car park. She was adamant we should carry on and we agreed that at the very least I'd do today's walk. The plan for this evening's entertainment in Hebden Bridge was that we would meet up with my brother and his wife who were driving out from their home in Manchester – if by then thoughts had changed and I was going to go home, leaving the Way with them would be easier.

**Duncan:** While Chris listened intently on the phone I had been exchanging meaningful glances with James. Rather than attempt to hear half a conversation I had retreated out of earshot so that Chris could consider what was being said without me in his eye-line.

I circled the car park, kicking stones. All the while the thought that the walk was for all intents over flooded over me. Although I knew that Mag's mum had been very unwell, the news was that she was thought to have turned a corner. Indeed, just the night before Chris had mentioned that one of the nursing staff at the home, who had many years of experience, was sure that she was on the mend. So not only did I not anticipate this awful event, I hadn't even considered it as a possibility.

Once the phone call was complete I was even more surprised that Chris did not take up James' offer to drive him to a railway station. Instead Chris headed across the road and I followed but how much further we would walk was very much in doubt.

**Chris:** So we bade farewell to James and set off on Day 3. As we did so, the weather was bright but the strong wind persisted. From the road we headed immediately onto a gravel track which soon gave way to an excellent path heading north along Millstone Edge. We had good views of the Castleshaw reservoirs in the near distance down the steep slope to our left but also beyond, to where the threatening cloud was building again. Soon the sun was completely gone and by the

**Enjoying the conditions on White Hill**

**The rocky path on Blackstone Edge**

time we reached the trig point at White Hill we had our rain gear on.

We crossed the motorway footbridge soon after and as we started the climb from there to Blackstone Edge, we were, just as we had been forty years ago, being lashed by hard rain that was driven in sideways at us from the west, to which we were totally exposed. Even though I was wearing several layers of expensive modern, allegedly waterproof clothing, we reached the White House pub on the A58 just as completely soaked through to the skin as we had been in '79. Water was even sloshing around inside my boots.

Back then, this had been the end of the second day and we had jumped on a bus for the shelter of a b&b in nearby Littleborough but today we were here in the middle of the day. The White House pub was, surprisingly, open, but we opted not to go in. Instead we pressed on around a series of reservoirs still completely exposed to the west,

**Blackstone Edge from the b&b, Littleborough**

from where the incessant wind and eventually intermittent rain continued to afflict us. It occurred to me that although I was perhaps as wet as I have ever been while walking, actually the level of saturation was not inducing misery. I was perhaps a little colder than I would have liked, but my feeling was, ok, I'm very wet, and although it is fairly unpleasant I will eventually be dry; and with that positive thought I was convinced that the weather, whatever it threw at us, would not be a reason for us to give up this walk.

There might be other reasons however. As we walked, both in my mind and in conversation with Duncan I was constantly turning over the go home or carry on conundrum. By now I was comforted by the knowledge that one of Mag's sisters, Teresa, had arrived from her home in Wales, having set off with her husband as soon as she'd received the news.

Mag is one of five fairly far flung siblings – brothers in Hampshire and Spain, sisters in Wales and Buckinghamshire – but she was in regular contact with them all and had let them know the sad news straight away. Teresa was already planning on staying several days and her husband had immediately and generously offered to drive to retrieve me from wherever I was at any time, but Mag was maintaining her intention that I keep on.

In the early afternoon I called my brother to confirm that we were on schedule for our Saturday evening rendezvous in Hebden Bridge and also broke the news about Brenda.

Slowly the idea was forming that I would carry on, but that I would at any time, if Mag wished, head straight home. She continued to say that she was 'fine' but who could know how that might change in the days ahead? For the last few years she had visited housebound and increasingly immobile Brenda at least once a day, and would only miss doing so on days when she knew that someone else was visiting. Even then she would probably drop in sometime during the day just to say hello and check if Brenda needed anything. She would spend time just chatting to her, do her hair and nails, read poetry to her and also, in recognition of their shared, strongly held Catholic faith, took Communion to her virtually every day. Brenda told anyone who would listen how blessed she was to have such a wonderful daughter – and I think she was right.

In recent years Mag and I had only taken holidays together at times when we knew that a sibling could come to stay in Saffron Walden, either in Brenda's house, or latterly after she'd moved into a nearby care home, in our house, for the whole duration of our time away. Mag had shown remarkable commitment to caring for her mum and that huge part of her life had just come to an end, not unexpectedly, but very abruptly. I could only wait to see how she might react to this momentous change and provide the necessary support if, when and in whatever way she needed it.

Not long after one o'clock, a little dryer by now, Duncan and I rounded the northern end of the Warland reservoir hopeful that one or other of the odd bits of blue that were starting to appear might herald a more pleasant afternoon. The impressive Stoodley Pike monument two or three miles in the distance, made it clear where we were headed. The path turned in a north easterly direction so at least the wind was at our backs, but it remained strong and on several occasions mischievous gusts got under our packs' rain covers. As they billowed out like parachutes above our heads we were glad that the manufacturers had cleverly fixed one end of the rain cover to the pack.

The blue stuff was increasing but we were still intermittently lashed with short bursts of rain, so we kept our wet weather gear on. To the west, great views of Calderdale opened up, to the town of Todmorden and somewhere down there the brilliantly named - it could only be in Yorkshire - hamlet of Mankinholes where the youth hostel provides a popular overnight stop for many Pennine Way walkers. As beautiful as the valley is, it is also prone to flooding and the settlements in this curve of the Calder from Todmorden, through Hebden Bridge, Mytholmroyd to Sowerby Bridge have experienced damaging floods in recent years, not least during Storm Ciara which battered the area a

few months after we passed through it.

This is a very popular walking area and in the slowly improving weather there were a good number of people out for a Saturday afternoon walk. The paths here are sometimes two or three people wide, sound underfoot and offer excellent walking. Many paths criss-cross these moors and join with the Pennine Way to head to the common destination of the monument which upon our arrival, thanks to its considerable girth, offered us at last a brief break from the wind and the still intermittent rain. The structure we learned, or probably re-learned, commemorates the end of war against Napoleon and has dominated this vista, in a couple of versions, for two hundred years. We took a few minutes rest and removed our wet weather gear in preparation for what we hoped would be a sunlit descent to the night's accommodation.

**The monument watches over the grand sweep of Calderdale**

Hebden Bridge lies about three miles ahead but even from the height of Stoodley Pike the town remains invisible due to its position in a deep, steep sided section of the Calder valley. The Way actually passes to the west of the town and forty years ago so did we, but this time an overnight stop here fits our schedule nicely and offers the promise of a variety of pub and restaurant venues for our meeting with Bernard and Linda.

The monument

It seems that in recent years there have been attempts to lure walkers off the main route at this point and into the town. Hebden Bridge Walkers Action have created and signposted the Hebden Bridge Loop, which we now followed for a short time. However, we had decided (actually I'm to blame: this is my scheduling) to stay not in the town but to camp at Old Chamber farm, situated just to the south, so after a few minutes we left the Loop and headed due east to the campsite.

**Duncan:** We were to hear later that evening that Hebden Bridge is a mecca for walkers due to being surrounded by a remarkable network of footpaths. Certainly the OS map for this area looks as though it has been close stitched with green thread. Despite the wind and occasional rain there were plenty of people about and we couldn't help but overhear snatches of conversation. A group of young women walked towards us and one of the group pointed at some sheep droppings while jokingly asking her friends,

'Where do you think this is on the Bristol Stool scale?'

They were closely followed by a young family, the father confidently telling his little boy,

'Edmund Hillary wore tweed on Everest.'

'What's tweed, daddy?'

Probably an example of the kind of specialist knowledge required to pass the eleven plus examination.

**Chris:** Old Chamber is at the same height as we were at this point, so the last bit of the walk was a level stroll. The sun was now shining brightly, we had plenty of time – it wasn't even three o'clock at this point – and we stopped for a few minutes to take pictures back towards the monument and down into Calderdale. As I turned to resume walking – aargh! – the knee thing returned. I had been relieved and encouraged that Day 2 had been completely free of trouble from the knee but now I was limping again and completed the last half mile in considerable pain. There seemed to be no particular reason why the pain should have returned: it hadn't been a particularly hard walking day, no massive climb or great distance. It had been very wet and we'd been cold at times but there'd been nothing really

**The delightful approach to Old Chamber**

extreme to cope with, but once again, lifting my right leg and bending the knee to take a step engendered searing pain. Thankfully there was just a short distance to go to the campsite but I made it there in considerable and worrying discomfort. I could only hope the pain would subside again and that it wouldn't prove to be the day's second reason to go home.

An hour or so later we were showered, tents pitched and in the campsite's Honesty Box catering facility, a shed with a kettle and coffee. While we enjoyed a warming cup, a highly incongruous eastern European lady struck up conversation with us. She seemed to share some common gardening interests with Duncan: I say seemed only because I found her accent utterly impenetrable. How Duncan managed this conversation I will never know.

On arrival at Old Chamber I'd called my brother to confirm arrangements for the evening's revelry and talked more about Brenda. He also immediately offered to collect me and take me home to be with Mag. 'If it was my wife I'd be going straight home' he told me, not really helping to support the view that when Mag said she was fine, I should believe her. 'The Pennine Way will still be there next year' he added. True, but Duncan and I had prepared for over a year to ensure that our sixty-three year old bodies would be up to it. The training was all about peaking in these late summer weeks. And as it turned out, although the Way is still there as I write, so is Covid 19, which at the very least would have seriously disrupted our plans.

I suggested to Duncan that we take a taxi into town, and a phone call and a short drive later we were strolling around the centre of Hebden Bridge. Once again I was relieved that my knee pain was easing, though I couldn't understand how or why it had afflicted me in the first place. We dropped into a Co-op supermarket to stock up on a few breakfast and lunchtime provisions for Day 4, and then went in search of a suitable pub.

By about seven o'clock we were in Calan's micropub, as the name suggests a tiny place but one with a fantastic selection of beers, exceptionally friendly clientele and a great ambience. Perusing a bar crammed with handpumps labelled with names of beers we'd not heard of let alone drunk, I plumped for a local, award winning porter. As I ordered, a voice piped up from behind congratulating me on my choice and we turned to greet Andy, local character and (perhaps) the only communist in the village. Wearing a Che Guevara style beret, complete with five point star, Andy was sitting at one of the high benches and was clearly ready for a chat. We joined him for an hour or so of delightful conversation about a multitude of topics which ending with us being invited to join the locals later on at one of the towns other pubs. This pub's special attraction was a terrace on which smoking took place – you know, *smoking*.

A steady stream of locals dropped into Calan's, all of whom greeted Andy, who in turn introduced us, and who then also fell into conversation with us. It was a wonderfully convivial couple of hours and I think the two of us will remember the evening as a standout of the 2019 expedition. The following day though, we would both recall the eerie similarity of Andy's mannerisms of speech and physical tics to those of our late friend Doug – at times it almost seemed like we were listening not to Andy but Doug holding forth in his characteristic fashion, all the time pushing his specs back up on to the bridge of his nose and picking at his beard.

Eventually Bernard and Linda arrived and conversation between he and I turned more serious as we discussed family matters, how Mag was doing and whether I should be going home. By now we were several pints in with more beer to accompany a pizza so I wonder whether I was making a logical argument for continuing the walk, though I was by now fairly sure I would. Bernard repeated that should things change at home and Mag feel she needed me, he'd come and pick me up and take me back to Essex. At the end of the evening, Linda kindly drove us back up the hill to Old Chamber where mercifully our tents were pitched closer to the toilet block than they had been at Edale.

*Chapter Six*

What a day it had been. Like forty years ago we had been soaked to the skin on Blackstone Edge but in pretty much any other way you care to think about it had been different. My thoughts and conversation had been dominated by the obvious issue and before starting the long struggle to get a decent night's sleep, I called Mag one more time. After this call I finally felt my decision to continue was the right one: she insisted she was comfortable with her siblings around her, helping with all the stuff that needs to be done when someone dies and that she'd actually be more unhappy if I gave up the

walk. With the proviso that I would come home if the funeral turned out to be while I was still away, we agreed that I would press on. And the knee was ok too.

**Stoodley Pike from the path to Old Chamber farm**

Mapping:
https://www.wikiloc.com/hiking-trails/pw-4-hebden-bridge-ickornshaw-40796393

**The not so mobile phone,**
**'Connecting you now, press button "A" caller'**

# Chapter 7 - Hebden Bridge to Ickornshaw

304 ft 17.39 mi

Total ascent: 7638 ft Total distance: 61.25 miles

September 1st

**Duncan**: There was no hint of a red dawn over the walkers' paradise of Hebden Bridge. The star-flecked night sky had given way to lumpen grey clouds that obscured the sun. Occasional fleeting shafts of sunlight illuminated the condensation inside the tent and the merest touch of the gossamer-like material was enough to cause a shower of icy droplets.

I unzipped the tent door that had all the colour, texture and charm of cold wilted lettuce and escaped to the great outdoors. It was seven o'clock, early for a Sunday and as I stretched my limbs I was glad that daylight had called time on a barely endurable night.

Inside the barn, where the extensive facilities were located, I inspected my washing which was dangling limply on a makeshift line. My shirts and undergarments had seemingly clung on to every molecule of water and so there was no option but to complete the drying process by using plan B. I regretfully changed into one of the wet shirts, underpants and socks and continued with the morning. Chris was also showing signs of life and his befuddled demeanour hinted that he too had endured an uncomfortable night. I wondered if Chris was having more serious thoughts of going home, if only to be back in a warm bed.

We headed to the Honesty Box for breakfast. The incongruous eastern European lady and her family from yesterday were no longer encamped on the makeshift seats devouring ice cream, so I didn't have to make small talk about the lack of local forestry and foraging opportunities. During that perplexing conversation, Chris had appeared to be lost in thought about his news and I, realising that I was unlikely to get any helpful utterances from him, was left to fend off the increasingly awkward questions from the grandmother of the clan, who for some unknown reason had formed the opinion that I held some responsibility for these issues.

I took the food that we'd bought in the Co-op the night before and made up a set of rolls, some for breakfast and the rest for lunch. We discussed plans, what to do when, as I saw it, the inevitable phone call would tip the balance and bring an end to the walk. I said I would stay on, not because I want to complete the Pennine Way on my own but because we were expecting company. A long planned meeting with our old friend Jerome, who'd dubbed himself 'the interloper'. He was to walk with us for two days and my thought was to fulfil the obligation before going home, because as Bernard had said the night before, 'the Pennine Way will always be here'. There was nothing to stop us returning to continue at a later date.

Although it would feel like a defeat.

Breakfast completed I returned to my tent. My next pitch neighbour was packing his kit away and I recognised the make of his tent. It was a 'Big Agnes' and was in a price range two or three times the cost of mine. For all that extra money you end up with less, in that you have less weight to carry.

I was well aware that we were early risers, so I offered a quiet 'Good morning' but he either didn't hear me or feigned not to. It's not my habit to force conversation on people so I let it pass.

My shirt had dried on my back so I braced myself to exchange it for the wet one left on the line, placing the now pleasantly dry shirt in my bag. The weather had an undecided look about it, the sun could shrug off the clouds and burn brightly or the clouds could thicken and bring rain, or both. Even for the weather gods, Sunday morning was no time for big decisions.

Big Agnes had packed and gone and around us the other tent

dwellers were rising to greet the day and what a glum, miserable bunch they were. So unlike the photographs of people that you see in the camping magazines, joyfully engaged in outdoor activities. I had imagined most campers to be irrepressible optimists, their character undimmed by a dank morning. Here the denizens had the downtrodden demeanour of people who'd made a seriously bad life choice several years ago and were now trapped in a long and desperate struggle to repay their debt.

Carefully I packed the contents of the tent into my sack. The last thing I had to deal with was the tent itself which was demonstrating its water repellent qualities by having a vast reservoir of twinkling droplets covering the exterior skin. The humidity was probably already one hundred percent despite the howling wind. There was no sun to encourage drying so I packed the sodden tent with my cold wet hands. I had up until this moment carried this inside my pack. Now I was wary of bringing so much wetness into close proximity with my

**Hebden Bridge from the campsite**

clothes and so I attached it to the straps on the outside.

It was nearly nine o'clock and around us campers were beginning to fill their cars with vast boxes of equipment. We shouldered our packs and left them to their misery, taking a path down into the valley, across a muddy field and through a wood, before entering the town. Chris's laminated sheet mentioned a cafe that opened early and we headed there for a real coffee.

A small black jackdaw hopped hopefully nearby as we drank our coffees on the terrace beside the river. It was close enough to reveal the grey and black markings on its head and its eye had a friendlier, warmer character than its crow cousins. I had seen a few about the town the night before but none had ventured as close as this.

Chris rang home one more time and on receipt of words of reassurance, we set off for the day. Hebden Bridge was a rainbow of grey as we traipsed through the town, passing the pub with the 'high terrace' that Andy was keen for us to visit, before starting the long walk out of the valley and back to the Pennine Way.

A bell rang and yet another group of cyclists laboured past us on the woodland by-way. I am sure that cyclists are unaware of just how silently they travel and a sudden 'ding-ding' made a few steps behind us generally caused us to jump out of our skins. Alternatively this could be just the reaction they were hoping for. It would be fairer to ring twice, once about twenty or so yards away to give us walkers a chance of realising what is about to happen. Cyclists however, are harbingers of rain, or at least they were today and as soon as they have passed us the sky darkened and the inevitable deluge followed.

Fortunately, unlike yesterday the taps were turned off not long afterwards and the sun came out as we reached the village of Colden and the Pennine Way. The path from here crosses muddy farmland that lack the flagstones which are a marker of the National Parks, so I found I was slipping and sliding along. Chris was seemingly unaffected by this muddy terrain. Before long we came to moorland and with it the howling wind which had not relented since the first day. Although the sun shone brightly, I was far from warm.

Below us in the valley I could see a reservoir which was where we were headed and hidden just beyond was a place that had a special meaning for us. Our younger selves reached this point at the end of the third day and we were so tired we could walk no further. In the valley just beyond the reservoir we pitched our tent on the only bit of lush green grass that we had seen for several miles. Just beyond this point is the Pack Horse Inn and we snuck up there for dinner before falling asleep in this magical place. Of course wild camping is not allowed in England and doubly so on water authority land so we were anxious that we would not be discovered.

**Our campsite at Graining Water**

**A series of lonely reservoirs**

My memory of this place is crystal clear and I was convinced that our photographs had only enhanced and reinforced it. Although Graining Water had not changed significantly since our last visit, the shifting sands of time have conspired to make the approach to our impromptu camping site and the walk to the Pack Horse Inn completely about face in my own mind. The only thing that was reassuringly similar was the inviting patch of grass and I am sure that many others have been lured to camp there since.

We left Graining Water and passed a series of lonely reservoirs as the Way climbed to cross a bleak moor. For the past hour or so the sun had been cheerfully warming us. As we reached the flat crest and looked down into the next valley we could pick out the old farmhouse, Top Withens, sheltered by a couple of gnarled trees. Beyond, ominous rain clouds skidded rapidly towards us. On arrival at the stone building, which is the most famous of several farmhouses

**Top Withens**

that are thought to be the inspiration for Heathcliff's home in Emily Brontë's book Wuthering Heights, the taps were turned on once again.

Fortunately there was a bench on the leeward side of Top Withens and we unhitched our backpacks before settling down to eat the lunch that I had prepared in the Honesty Box earlier. From our sheltered vantage point the heavy rain drops shot over our heads as we surveyed the surrounding land.

What a desperate place to build a farmhouse. The crumbling dry stone walls enclosed fields of bog and moorland. No crops could prosper here and even sheep would merely survive, with little prospect that they might fatten up for market. The rough stone farmhouse has crumbled over time but part of the old building has been renovated and inside there is now a bothy for walkers, which must be a great relief in poor weather.

The rain relented and we headed off down the track past some tourists who were making the pilgrimage up from Haworth. For the first time today we started to consider the evening's accommodation options. The laminated plan was to camp at the next stopping point but we didn't sleep well last night and the weather forecast was not promising. Also, we recalled that our host James from the first b&b had dubbed this campsite as 'midge heaven'.

We do know that we are going to meet up with the interloper and have a meal before he goes off to the enviable comfort of his b&b. We were cold, wet and tired and the idea of another similar night was not inviting. The option of staying in a b&b was a welcome thought. What if there was a room in the b&b where the interloper is staying? What if we stayed two nights and therefore could walk without our full packs for a day? Never mind the what ifs, let's ask him.

Before we do, it is time to find out some more about the interloper and to do that we need to go back in time.

**Chris**: All of our walking buddies – Bill, Steve, Jonathan and Jerome – had suggested that they might join us for a day or two at some stage, but Jerome was the only one who carried out the threat. The three of us however were the 'A team' reunited, with friendship going back to before Duncan and I had conquered the Way the first time.

**Duncan**: Our photography course was a remnant from before the Polytechnic was formed when Walthamstow was a college of art (most famous alumni; musicians Viv Stanshall of the Bonzo Dog Doo Dah Band, Ian Dury, who was yet to break through, and film director Peter Greenaway). It was probably a very expensive course to run and the powers that be decided that our year was to be the last intake. The winding down of the course coincided with the Polytechnic's decision to move the arts faculty from Walthamstow to Plaistow for the start of what would be our third and final year and so it was necessary for us students to find new accommodation, or commute.

Chris was asking around for people to get together to share a student house. I was sharing two rooms with Desmond, another guy on the course but he, lucky boy, decided he was going to spend the next year with his girlfriend, so I was up for a new place to live.

**Chris**: By the end of the second year I already had Duncan and yet another photography student John signed up. I let the Poly's accommodation service know that we had one more vacancy and they alerted Jerome, who duly contacted me during the summer break. He seemed like a decent chap, and he was happy with the rent and the description I offered of the Leytonstone terrace which was to be our home for the foreseeable future. We agreed that he would move in come late September. It did occur to me though, that if he was to join us there, he would probably have to be barred from calling himself Jerome.

**Duncan**: Yes, I did feel that his renaming to Jerry was a bit harsh but he made no complaint.

When we fetched up at the new house at the end of September, we were all curious about our new resident whose belongings had arrived in an object of wonder. In his room was a huge wooden trunk with

**Tidy and neat with eye-catching décor like all student accommodation**

the letters JADW stencilled on the top, as if it had materialised from a Jennings and Darbishire book. Jerome was nowhere to be seen so we had an opportunity to appraise our new home. The house itself was a classic Edwardian east end terrace that was untouched by modernity. There was just one electric fan heater for the whole house. The water closet was located outside, protected from the worst of the weather by a rickety veranda. During our visits to the toilet we could enjoy the view across the garden which was in the process of re-wilding. It is difficult to believe but this was a palace in comparison to my previous accommodation.

**Chris**: Convening at the London E11 address in time for the start of term we hit it off pretty quickly. By we I mean Duncan, Jerome and me – John liked to remain fairly aloof, but the three of us were soon sharing budgets, cooking duties, trips to the pub and women. Actually that last bit is untrue: Jerome was, despite being so much younger and of course far less mature than his new housemates, already fixed up with the delightful Julie, to whom he remains married to this day. In fact there's a bit of a tale about that.

**Jerome is wearing 'Army Surplus' by Lawrence Corner**

**Duncan**: One day Chris received a letter and when Jerome had left for college, he called the rest of us together and divulged the contents. Jerome, it turned out, had a girlfriend who was still at school in Devon. She had reason to be in London soon and wanted to turn up and surprise Jerome over a weekend. All we had to do was make it happen.

The morning before we hoovered and tidied the house up as much as we could and Chris went into 'father of the house mode' telling Jerome that he needed to spruce up a bit, have a bath, launder his bedding, that kind of thing. At tea-time, there was a knock on the front door and we had engineered the room so that Jerome was nearest the door and first to open it. Jerome's face was a picture and he was unable to utter sentences for several minutes. We all liked Julie and she was pleased that we had worked hard to make her plan a reality. They had a great time and Jerome was almost unable to believe that this had happened.

**Chris**: Jerome says now that he realised he was 'one of us' when one day, all four residents presented at the local branch of Radio Rentals. The plan was to hire a cheap telly for the year in an attempt to reduce our unsustainable pub expenditure. When the man asked for someone to sign all the paperwork and take responsibility for the payments, Jerome relates that Duncan and I gripped him before taking a choreographed step backwards, leaving the aloof one standing at the desk being handed a pen.

**Duncan**: Anyway, back to the pressing concern of tonight's accommodation. Chris was on the phone and put the idea to Jerome. At this moment we had no knowledge of where he was staying, all we did know was that he was on his way. Within a few minutes he called back and confirmed that the b&b is booked for two nights and he will pick us up from Ickornshaw in an hour or so. We continued the walk with a spring in our step and the weather decided to lay off the wet stuff for a while.

Sliding down the green farmland into Ickornshaw, we spotted

Jerome's car pootling along a back road from the village. It was good to see our friend and with the added promise of a dry night in a warm bed, life had a decidedly rosy hue.

The b&b that Jerome had booked turned out to be in Malham. This place also has a campsite which Chris had noted on our laminated sheet as the venue for the next evening's stay. It is with some relief that we swerved the wet grass and entered the b&b. We removed our boots in the large warm porch in the centre of which was a clothes horse, groaning under the weight of other walkers' sodden garments. We were shown to our bedroom and immediately laid out our wet clothes on the various surfaces, which soon released an interesting and not entirely pleasant fug into the air.

After a shower and change of clothing we headed across the road to the Buck Inn, where forty years previously we had rested after an extremely wet morning avoiding flooding on the River Aire. I don't remember much about this place as I was also experiencing a cramping stomach ache that was so bad I had to just lie on the bed, though I do recall the bedroom being very bare.

Although it was Sunday evening, the Buck was still offering the lunchtime roast dinner menu, which seemed a natural choice as it would be different from the usual pub classics that had made up our diet so far. We sat down in the beautifully restored wood panelled dining area and Jerome began to tell us some surprising and extraordinary news. For some time the firm that he worked for had been seeking new ownership as the present owners were reaching retirement age. They'd nearly succeeded in completing a sale a couple of years earlier but it had eventually come to nothing. Since then there had been rumours of further interest but on the previous Friday, Jerome received a phone call summoning him to the head office in Scotland as there was to be an announcement. Jerome's response was to point out that he had a couple of days holiday booked which he was not willing to change and instead he travelled up to meet us.

Chris told Jerome the news about about the death of his mother-in-law and I could tell that Jerome was as surprised as me that Chris was still here.

I looked at my friends and wondered, since circumstance had so obviously conspired against us how it was possible for the three of us to be sitting around this table.

**They're reet friendly up north!**

Mapping:
https://www.wikiloc.com/hiking-trails/pw-5-ickornshaw-to-malham-40811313

What James Bond drives around his farm.
This was actually made by (*the same company that makes*) Aston Martin

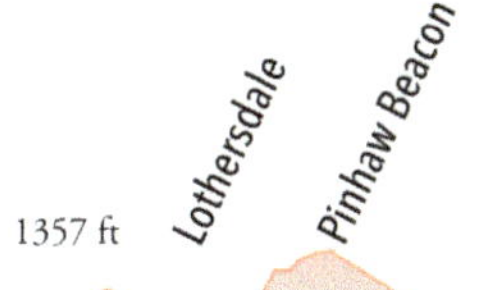


Gargrave

Malham

# Chapter 8 - Ickornshaw to Malham

387ft

17.92 mi

Total ascent: 9603 ft

Total distance: 79.17 miles

September 2nd

**Chris:** On our return to the accommodation at Malham late in the afternoon of Day 5, the old boy at the house was busying himself in the drying room. He asked me where we'd walked today and I explained that we'd been driven to Ickornshaw first thing and walked back from there.

'Ickornshaw? You've walked from Ickornshaw?' he asked seeking confirmation of a feat that appeared to be beyond his understanding of the possible. 'By…' he continued after a moment's consideration, aghast, gazing off into the middle distance and gently shaking his head. Then as though to confirm his bafflement, he said 'By...' again. I in turn, was baffled by his apparent belief that what we'd done was so remarkable. Certainly, the day's walk had been one of the longer days on our itinerary at the best part of eighteen miles, but once the climb to the highest point at Pinhaw Beacon, just over twelve hundred feet and all over in the first five miles was done, the going was easy, much of it low level with generally good conditions underfoot. Also, as is the case with much of the Way, the daily start and finish points suggest themselves: many people must have walked exactly the same stage and even opted to stay at this b&b, so surely the old boy must have heard of people doing this before. Still, it was good to know he was impressed.

He wasn't around as we'd assembled for breakfast, but his wife was. She looked out of the window at the grey sky and the washing being blown horizontal on the line. With the authority of someone possessed of a sixth sense as far as the dales and its weather are concerned, she issued a prediction that was very welcome: 'You'll be alright today'. That was good to know. A few minutes later their son came bustling through the dining room. 'You're gunna get wet again today lads' he warned, with certainty equal to that of his mother. This man, we had learned, was actually a professional rugby union referee. We laughed at the conflicting meteorological opinion, but suspected that it would turn out that of course, the ref is always right.

The ref was also our driver to Ickornshaw. While we enjoyed another excellent breakfast he busied himself around the place, telling us at one point that he wouldn't be able to leave for probably another thirty minutes. We settled in for another relaxed cup of coffee but mystifyingly, seconds later he was back in the dining room announcing that he'd be ready to go in five. Cue mad dash to get organised - we'd better not delay him - and we were soon on the road heading south to Ickornshaw.

It was pleasing to have Jerome's company for this couple of days. At the start of that final college year when he'd entered our lives, Duncan and I weren't particularly close. We were on different strands of the photography course and so had spent little academic time together in the first two years. Our social lives hadn't overlapped much either. We definitely had enough in common to settle in comfortably together though: we were both football and music fans, shared a similar sense of humour, enjoyed pubs and beer and were very similar in age, education and backgrounds.

Post college, we both worked for a number of years at Bart's Hospital in London so kept well in touch. By coincidence, we both left permanent employment in the mid-eighties to set up our own businesses, or at least in my case to join the business set up by Mag, who I'd married a couple of years earlier. There was a degree of overlap in the photography based work our two companies were doing and we would occasionally come together to work on a particular job, so we remained in contact and our friendship persisted.

Jerome meanwhile, had married the aforementioned Julie soon after leaving college and they had left the UK to work overseas. Contact with them throughout this period became sporadic to say the least, but in the early noughties, Jerome got back in contact with us both. He and Julie were intending, he told us, to renew their wedding vows, twenty-five years after the initial event. Duncan and I had both been at that shindig – indeed, Duncan was best man – and they wanted us both there this time too.

We of course attended and the three of us agreed to meet up again in the near future for a pint or two. Those pints were duly consumed a few weeks later and in the accompanying conversation we decided that we should get together in some probably mountainous location for a few days of walking, drinking and serious catching up. I put forward the possibility of staying in a farmhouse in Spain owned by Mag's brother. Situated in the western Pyrenees, the farmhouse is on the side of a wonderfully tranquil valley, a beautiful place with endless opportunity to walk on excellent mountain paths straight out of the

**The western Pyrenees, where we rediscovered walking**

door. The subsequent five day excursion there in May '04 was the first of the annual walking trips that would, more than a dozen years on, find us in the Sierra Nevada discussing the Pennine Way.

So, on with our first Pennine Way day as a trio. As we drove toward Ickornshaw the three of us made forays into small talk with the ref but these attempts were generally short lived, his conversational style being limited to fairly short, firm statements that allowed no space for follow up comment or discussion. What he said went. Odd that he should become a rugby referee.

He dropped us right where the Way crossed the A6808, exactly where we'd left the path yesterday and we headed off on the first of today's eighteen miles. Jerome was fairly anxious about this distance, feeling less prepared for it than we were but we reassured him that it was fairly benign, mostly low level walking. In the folklore of our walking group, Jerome's presence is held to be a harbinger of fine weather but his powers were only partially working this morning, the sun shining intermittently as we walked over the rolling countryside of this lovely part of Yorkshire. We noted however that the ever

**Spot the difference: Lothersdale in 1979**

present wind was - of course - bringing in threatening clouds from the west.

The paths were easy to follow but generally narrow as we were managed through farmland, except when the Way unusually followed short stretches of rural road, happily containing very little traffic. As the path reached the top of each undulation delightful vistas opened up, revealing some small settlement or farm in the next valley, criss-crossed by miles of dry stone walls and with vast skies above. The village of Lothersdale and the hundred and seventy year old tower of its former mill features in one of these vistas and is also a destination along the Way as the path drops again to pass through the village. This quiet place was once a thriving industrial community, the mill having a long history of commerce and the production of various commodities, notably textiles until well into the twentieth century. It would be a perfect stop for a rest and a pint, but we passed through the village before opening time, and there remained a lot of miles still to walk.

**and 2019**

**Duncan:** In the intervening years, Chris and I had once travelled up to this part of England and found ourselves looking wistfully across the Pennine landscape that Chris has just described. To explain, we were working on a video programme. When Chris went freelance he would join the crew of my video production company to work on various video programmes, initially on sound. The director I was working with at that time had found a full time post and I needed someone else. I had tried directing but I didn't feel it was the best use of my abilities, but Chris felt confident enough by that stage to give it a try. I really wanted this to work and Chris took to directing like he had been born to it. For a few years Chris became the director and I went back to being the cameraman and producer.

This day we had travelled up to Cowling, a village next to Ickornshaw on the route of the Pennine Way to interview a farmer about his health problems. We aimed to build a rapport with the old boy while filming him out and about on his farm, caring for his animals and doing a few odd jobs before interviewing him. I was following him when he decided to head into his chicken shed to collect some eggs for his lunch. I hadn't prepared for the smell and once back outside I had to take several deep breaths of fresh air to recover, while we surveyed the glorious view.

He was quite a character and extremely miffed that his farm, which was firmly in Yorkshire when he was born, had in amongst the baffling boundary changes of 1974 been roped into Lancashire. He was adamant that we should be aware that he was a Yorkshireman, born and bred. This important consideration noted, his interview was good value and Chris put him at ease while teasing out the history of his medical problems in amongst anecdotes about tuppin' sheep and winning rosettes at the local show. As we were wrapping up we asked him what his secret was. How did he manage with all the tasks that he had to do everyday? He tapped his nose and replied, 'Ah don't smoke, Ah don't drink and Ah don't mess wi' women.'

His farm was only a stone's throw from Lothersdale and on the journey back to the hotel, we detoured to drive slowly through the village, both of us wishing that we had brought our walking boots.

**Chris:** Lothersdale is also the start of the day's biggest effort, a climb from about six hundred feet to Pinhaw Beacon at just over twelve hundred feet, but not a particularly onerous couple of miles. We were walking light too: as we were returning to the same accommodation as last night we were able to leave most of our stuff at the b&b, which meant it really was pretty easy. In retrospect, I wonder whether the chance to walk with just a 'day sack', which we did on four occasions all told, helped to make the whole enterprise a bit easier than it might have been, or at least less demanding than it was forty years ago.

At around the point the path turns more or less due west across Elslack Moor, we were joined from seemingly nowhere by a be-wellingtoned Compo-like figure and his dog.

'Pennine Wayin'?' he asked. We confirmed that indeed we were.

'Ah'll walk wi' yer', he announced and fell in alongside us on the wide path across the heather clad landscape. From the top of the moor he pointed out the Lancashire settlements of Earby, and a little further

**Windswept on Pinhaw Beacon**

away, Barnoldswick, where he lived. Our temporary companion clearly loved the moors and in a wide ranging conversation he revealed that he had himself done the Pennine Way in his younger day. We were interested to hear his experience and impressed that he had apparently made Kirk Yetholm in six days!

'An' yer know what I'm gunna tell yer, don't yer?' he continued.

We didn't.

'We turned rahnd, 'n' come back in seven.'

Mmmm. More than forty miles a day for thirteen consecutive days? I'm not sure we believed him or if he expected us to, but we were reminded that in 1979 we met two guys who were *running* the Pennine Way, north to south with just the lightest of light tents, a water bottle and an intention to complete the journey in just four days. Who knows? Maybe our new pal really had achieved this great feat.

All too soon though we had to bid him farewell as he branched off to where his car was parked on a small road that crossed the moor. He wished us well and pointed out where the next few miles of the Way would take us, as we headed off the moor toward Thornton-in-Craven. By now any hint of sunshine had deserted us and rainwear had been donned all round.

As we walked we heard more about the employment uncertainty that Jerome was suffering. It wasn't certain that things would turn out ideally and he was clearly concerned, but hoping for clarity later in the day, as an announcement regarding the future was imminent.

The rest of the day's walk continues at low level all the way to Malham, through pleasant though not especially interesting farmland, and is not hard work in any sense. Soon after passing through Thornton-in-Craven the path joins the Leeds and Liverpool Canal and follows the towpath for a while, upon which the eye-catching double arch bridge at East Marton is a highlight. Leaving the canal we headed north east towards Gargrave where unusually for the Pennine Way, a pub presented itself for a lunchtime stop: a fairly late lunch but we were all ready for a sit down out of the rain and gloom that Day 5 had by now descended into.

The Mason's Arms we found, provided an excellent steak sandwich and good beer and was friendly and warm. Jerome took the opportunity to phone the office for updates, while Duncan and I reflected that by the standards of 1979, we were half a day behind. We had actually camped at Gargrave at the end of Day 4 back then, having had slightly longer Days 2 and 3. The following day we awoke to one of the few rainy days we had in '79, and the weather had deteriorated further as the morning went on. The walk from Gargrave soon joins

**Leeds and Liverpool Canal now (top) and then**

**'By... you've walked from Ickornshaw?' Arriving into Malham**

the River Aire and follows it to Malham, but that year the river was flooded and we were forced to divert and walk most of the last few miles on the road. We arrived in Malham in the early afternoon, very, very wet and as Duncan was also feeling unwell we decided to check in to the Buck Inn, and walked no further that day. That short day back then meant that by the end of today's walk here in 2019 we would be matching the '79 schedule.

As it happens, in places the Aire had broken its banks this time too, but nowhere near as extensively and we were able to walk along the river without problem. The rain continued however, not heavily but constantly and by the time we neared Malham the three of us were soggy, cold, and glad the walk was over.

Warmed and rested we repaired to Malham's other pub, the Lister Arms where more excellent food and beer was consumed and we enjoyed the company of Rob, who we'd first met back in Crowden. Though a day behind us at that point, he was aiming at a somewhat quicker completion of the two hundred and seventy miles than us and

I was surprised that by now he hadn't gained more than just the one day on us. He had some long days planned though so we thought this would be the last we'd see of him. Later we realised Simon was also in the next room, so more agreeable chat was had, though we were sad to learn that his other half Wendy had retired injured.

Duncan and I had to feel happy with our progress so far. We were perfectly on schedule and had to be pleased that we were keeping up with our 1979 progress, and feeling strong and confident despite the much poorer weather we were experiencing this time. Happily too, I had suffered no more symptoms from the intermittently troublesome knee and I was also comforted to hear from home that Mag was still feeling ok and pleased by our progress.

Perhaps the only way in which things were not going to plan so far was in terms of the cost: our stay in the Malham b&b, whilst reasonably priced was obviously much more expensive than the camping that had been planned. However, after Malham, with the exception of the odd bunkhouse or 'pod' we were anticipating camping every night, so we decided the indulgence while Jerome was visiting was justified.

At the end of Day 5 then, despite the vaguely unpleasant ambience of drying walking gear, we were happy to collapse into our warm room and comfortable beds in preparation for tomorrow's walk to Horton-in-Ribblesdale.

Mapping:
https://www.wikiloc.com/hiking-trails/pw-6-malham-horton-in-ribblesdale-40857283

The siren call of the Lister Arms

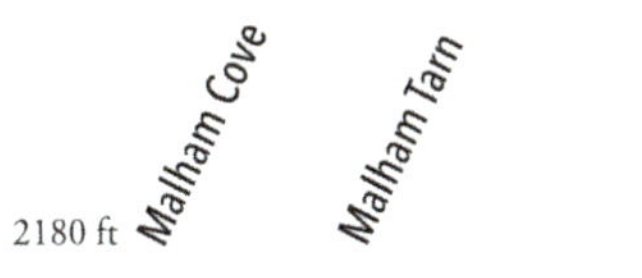

# Chapter 9 - Malham to Horton-in-Ribblesdale

Total ascent: 11539 ft Total distance: 92.34 miles

September 3rd

**Duncan:** The sky was sulking above the little limestone village of Malham. Although we had no particular plan for the coming evening, a day of rain was going to make any idea of sleeping in a tent thoroughly unappealing. Here in this cosy b&b, it was warm, it had good facilities and staff who could be friendly if they were given enough warning.

The place had been empty apart from a couple of other guests, so if one of the owners would be up for picking us up this evening and taking us back the next morning to Horton-in-Ribblesdale, we decided that we would be delighted to stay another night. This happy idea was quickly squashed by our host with the stinging authority of his rugby refereeing past, as if he was firmly rejecting an appeal from a cheeky player, as he stated that the place was fully booked. We trudged the obligatory ten yards back to our room.

Over breakfast we told Jerome of our failed plan and he, resourceful as ever, hatched another one. Jerome suggested that he could drive to Horton this morning and leave his car there, if one of our hosts can bring him back to Malham. That way, we could leave our belongings in the back of Jerome's car and walk with light packs again. This idea had a lot of merit because today's walk included Pen-y-Ghent, which although only a short climb is at the same time very steep and hopefully with less weight on my back I might avoid another jelly legged moment like the first day in the gully of Grindsbrook.

This will all take time as the roads meander amongst the hills so having secured agreement, Jerome rushed his breakfast to leave us early to complete the first stage of the plan. Meanwhile we waited in the porch and watched as the weather hovered between moist and wet. There was another phone call from home for Chris but the urgency seemed to have receded as members of Mag's family were rallying around. For me, it was beginning to feel as though the black cloud that had dogged us since Standedge was finally retreating.

On Jerome's return, which was achieved in a much quicker time than we had anticipated as it seemed the locals can outpace Formula 1 drivers along the winding roads, we donned our wet weather gear and braced ourselves to head out into the drizzle. Yet again we had received opposing weather forecasts for the day ahead from the owners of the b&b. Jerome, who had driven back from Horton with the father was optimistically told that the weather would brighten up, whereas the rugby refereeing son had glumly informed us while we sat in the porch observing the low clouds, that it would worsen.

**Below and opposite: the wrong way to the Cove**

Passing the Lister Arms, we took a path north of Malham which rose quickly to present a view across Malham Beck with the Cove slightly hidden ahead, partially curtained by a hump of green pasture. We'd taken the wrong path and a quick perusal by Chris of the OS map confirmed that we could carry on. Except that on all the gates that we had passed through there were well-made carved wooden signs that explicitly stated that there was no way across the beck to access the cove. It was a long way back and ahead the hump of green pasture steadfastly refused to reveal whether a bridge marked on the OS map existed or not. We pressed on until finally to our relief, a stone built bridge presented itself below us. The stones looked like they had been there forever and I was reminded of Tarr Steps on Exmoor, a clapper bridge which is claimed to be over three thousand years old but has to be remade by volunteers every time there is a major flood. Maybe a similar thing happens here.

On the other side of the beck, a carefully graded path took us to the bottom of the cove. Malham Cove is a spectacular feature but the real show was thousands of years ago at the end of the last ice age, when a

**A carefully graded path that even Chris can negotiate**

torrent of water cascaded over the edge, which is higher than the falls in Niagara. For now the waterfall sleeps, awakening only in the aftermath of fierce storms when it gives a ghostly impression of its past glories.

I have yet to see a photograph that does the cove justice as the trees in the valley, far from giving a sense of scale, seemed to shrink the limestone walls. Maybe a drone could capture the scene with more drama. However I doubt the National Park would allow such an intrusion.

The Pennine Way headed upward on a set of steps, passing a gate with yet another sign, which although initially humorous for us was, on reflection, a matter of life and death for others. The top of Malham

**Clints and grykes**

Cove is two hundred and sixty feet above the level of the river bed and the face of the old waterfall is perpendicular, so there is little chance of being caught on a ledge. It is achingly sad that anyone is desperate enough to contemplate such a fate.

For us the danger was merely walking across the treacherously worn limestone at the edge of the old waterfall. Resembling a series of rows of severely impacted molars, the clints (the top of the worn stones) and grykes (the eroded clefts between them) required all our concentration to progress along the path.

I believe the authorities won't allow a crossing of Malham Cove unless these terms are memorised, but clints and grykes sounds like a team of Yorkshire crime busters. Clints is the craggy-faced action hero and Grykes, the white coated boffin with hidden depths. The love interest could be the sultry Malham Tarn. Coming to you soon once Channel Five have worked out how to insert a veterinary surgery into the plot. I want a finder's fee, by the way.

**The dry valley**

From the top of the cove we turned to walk along the dry valley, where water once rushed to the edge of the falls. The ground had changed from the slippery mud of farmland, which had been with us since Hebden Bridge, to the firm grassy pasture of limestone country. The terrain is without doubt some of the best encountered on the whole Pennine Way. To celebrate, the weather had settled to dull with the occasional spit of rain and we were even sheltered from the strong wind in this steep sided valley.

Within half an hour we were in sight of Malham Tarn. The stream that leaves it vanishes into the ground after a couple of hundred yards at a place called Water Sinks. Instead of bubbling up under the cove, it reappears at Aire Head, a half a mile or so south of Malham. One can only wonder at the labyrinthine system of water filled caves beneath our feet.

Of course I am writing this as if I know all about it. As if, in some imaginary world, a couple of weeks before the walk we had travelled up to Malham with a bucket of fluorescein and a network of friends watching over the various streams downhill. Whereas, in truth I have just searched online and read a school science project. (Farsley Fairfield year 5 blog, since you ask. Primary school, it's just about my level of understanding when it comes to geology.)

Jerome mentioned that he came to Malham a few years back and did part of this walk on his own. He had printed out a paper map but he lacked proper wet weather gear and it was his bad fortune that the constant rain caused the ink to run and finally the paper to dissolve by the time he reached the Tarn. Fearing that he may never be seen again if he retraced his steps, he returned to Malham by walking along the road.

The wind had found us in the open and was letting us know that it hadn't gone away. The cloud sank to almost within touching distance and my money was now firmly on the ref's forecast for the day. Despite the gloomy prospect, the grassy path was a joy to walk along

**Malham Tarn**

and quickly we reached yet another gate. Here, an elderly gentleman driving a rather splendid all terrain mobility scooter was being ushered through by his partner from the confines of the lakeside path, and he chose this moment to see what his newly acquired drive could do.

He dramatically spun the steering wheel and headed off piste across the grassy common. His partner followed in his wake, calling plaintively, worried that some unseen sinkhole might claim him.

There was some respite for us from the wind and rain as we headed round behind the big house on the Tarn and through a wood. Beyond was barren moor and the weather declared open season on us walkers.

Our next staging post was Fountains Fell, a steady climb from the haven of Malham Tarn. We reached the top around one o'clock with the help of some biscuits from the interloper. It was the only help we were getting because everything else seemed to be against us. In the gathering cloud the two stone men at the top of Fountains Fell turned their backs on us. At the same time the pelting rain was being heavily lashed into us by the driving wind. Yes, this was walking but without any pleasure.

As we descended we could begin to see across the valley and ahead of us there was a thick blanket of cloud totally obscuring Pen-y-Ghent.

**The interloper on Fountains Fell exclusively styled by Maya Sport, Saint-Jean-Pied-de-Port**

Pen-y-Ghent (really)
Visibility: zilch. Windspeed: hooley. Precipitation: pelting.
Conditions: ideal!

Reasons to be cheerful? Er, none come to mind

Wainwright wrote in his book of the Coast to Coast Walk that, 'There's no such thing as bad weather, only unsuitable clothing'. At this moment I would like to take him into a walking and hiking store to view the section of clothing intended to cope with high winds, driving rain and fog. Maybe he could point out to me the items that would make this more bearable because I must have missed them when I was buying my kit.

What happened next needs some explanation. The rain was heavy, the wind was pushing a constant fifty miles an hour and although Chris and I are hardy(ish) walkers who know what is coming because we have already crossed the top of Pen-y-Ghent, we were aware that our companion had not had anything like our preparation.

We do know it will be a steep climb, one that would be sapping of our energy. We were also aware that for Jerome, tomorrow is going to be a very strange day when he would need all his wits about him as he returned to work. All this was known but it wasn't discussed. What we did talk about was a route that could be taken in terrible weather to avoid the worst of this. A route that forty years earlier was offered as a bad weather alternative to the Pennine Way. A route that is actually much more direct than the extreme dog leg that the Way follows over the mountain top and right here at the foot of the climb it was obvious that none of us much relished the prospect of a dangerous and ultimately fruitless traverse of Pen-y-Ghent.

So we didn't.

Of course, this is controversial. There are some people on, let's call it 'the Walking Spectrum', who would traverse Antarctica on two frostbitten stumps and might raise an eyebrow at our decision. At the other end of the same spectrum are those who drive to beauty spots to eat sandwiches and take in the view from the car.

Just for a moment let us imagine that they should meet. Let's say a car dwelling couple have ventured down to the South Pole to take in

**Opposite: Pen-y-Ghent in '79. If you can't see it, leave it, it's not worth it**

the view. As they sit opening their Thermos, Sir Ranulph Fiennes (*other explorers are available*) struggles by with a fully laden sled. The couple turn to each other, chink their plastic cups and say, 'Nutter'. Meanwhile Sir Ranulph wipes back an icicle and surveys them with a gimlet eye and thinks, 'Lightweights'.

Extreme though this example may be, everyday when walkers meet they are assessing each other and coming to similar conclusions.

As fully paid up members of the Lightweights fraternity, we turned our back on the shrouded summit of Pen-y-Ghent and instead headed down a broad byway, flanked by dry stone walls that took a more direct route to the small village of Horton-in-Ribblesdale. It was with considerable relief that we crossed the threshold of the Golden Lion Hotel at around three thirty in the afternoon. Especially as Jerome had parked his car there earlier in the day, so we could be reunited with our belongings.

We stood in the lobby and took off our soaking wet gear, causing rivulets of water to course across the flagstone floor. We left sopping wet footprints from our waterlogged socks as we walked into the tap room. Under the stern gaze of a poster of Sean Dyche, the fearsome Burnley manager, we ordered coffees and then asked the landlord about the accommodation choices, which turned out to be more than we had anticipated because as well as offering b&b there was a cheaper option that we had yet to experience. Aware that we had planned to be in the tent this evening, thereby saving money, especially after the luxury of the two extra nights in Malham, we decided to check out the delights of the bunkhouse.

The landlord took us outside around to some steps that led up from the car park to a room that was a riot of pine wood, kitted out like a Scandinavian sauna. Here there were five triple decker bunk beds with just enough space to negotiate our way around them. Beside the entrance there was a small side window and in the ceiling one Velux vibrating from the insistent drumming of the heavy rain. The manager mentioned that there were two toilets and showers in the adjoining

bathroom and we should be aware that the bunkhouse is unisex.

## A riot of pine

Nobody else was booked in this evening, we would have it to ourselves and for this reason, and this reason alone, we decided to give it a try. Putting the tent up in what by now would be the Horton-in-Ribblesdale water park and campsite was not an option worthy of discussion.

A few moments later, having spread our sodden clothes across a number of the plastic covered mattresses, it was a pleasure to enjoy the hot water of a shower. After the terrible conditions outside I lingered long in the warm flow before reluctantly towelling down and changing into something dry. Thus it was about an hour later that we rejoined a gently steaming Jerome basking in the warmth of a wood burning stove in the more convivial lounge bar.

From various work colleagues he was getting a jumbled and incoherent picture of the dramatic changes that were afoot. Despite the lack of clarity he did at least feel more prepared for his journey to the Scottish headquarters of his firm. He was unaware of his fate but sanguine about the days ahead.

We ordered a beer and some pork scratchings for much needed calories and sat down close to the warm stove. Meanwhile the regulars came in from their work and noisily sank several rounds of beer at the bar.

A food menu had been left on our table, and one of the advantages of knowing Jerome is that after decades of working in the food services industry he had the uncanny skill of instantly recognising when the claim of 'home cooking' was being stretched. To his experienced eye the menu was full of items that tallied with the ready microwaveable and deep fried meal options that were available from one of the big national suppliers. It was an easy decision to head to the other pub in the village and see what they had on offer. Outside, the rain was still pounding down so we hopped into Jerome's car for the half mile trip, passing a forlorn and sodden campsite on the way.

The other pub was the Crown Inn and on entering we saw a few of the friendly faces from the night before. Sitting around the cosy bar were Rob and Simon, Robin, an American and the occupant of 'Big Agnes' and a Father and Son partnership. We settled down for a pleasant evening. Of course the conversation turned to the weather and our fellow companions revealed that all of them had, despite the atrocious conditions, followed the Pennine Way to the letter and gone over the top of Pen-y-Ghent.

We questioned their sanity. (Nutters.)

We didn't feel the need to do it. We had, as I have already said, climbed Pen-y-Ghent on a gloomy dry day (even though Chris apparently didn't believe it - and why he would forget this is beyond me) and the views were lovely. The path down to Horton was a bit of a drag forty years ago and although I would like to have taken the detour to see the entrance to Hull Pot, we didn't then and there was no way we would have done so today. Finally to those who walked over Pen-y-Ghent in today's weather, we pointed out that Mountain Rescue would not have been too thrilled if they'd required help, so maybe they should consider the options more carefully in future.

Despite our protestations it was obvious they were unimpressed by our detour (Lightweights) because they are walkers, built to endure, whereas we walk for the enjoyment. I was drawn back to my childhood memories of youth hosteling and my conclusion that I 'was not of that ilk' was reinforced once more.

We ordered some food as it was genuinely home-made. Jerome and I ordered a beef madras curry, a strangely English concoction which, as his daughter had once remarked, 'only a heathen country can make'. The beer was good and the chat continued.

The night before in the pub in Malham, Rob had talked about his athletics past and had let slip a time for a long distance run in which he had competed. Jerome had memorised this and looked it up. It was in fact a remarkably fast time and Jerome suggested that Rob was rubbing shoulders with elite athletes, something that we could tell caused Rob a little swelling of pride. Because of this it looked as though his ambitious schedule would be well within his abilities.

Our food arrived and the portions were huge, which was just as well as we had been fuelled by biscuits alone today. Chris had ordered a liver dish and it too was presented on an enormous plate. The hot food and the beer mellowed the atmosphere.

The Father and Son partnership turned out to be walking from Land's End to John O'Groats. They had hit upon the Pennine Way as an unambiguous route to take them up the central spine of northern England and on to the border. Robin was cautious with his conversation and mainly listened on the edge.

It was starting to get dark and Jerome needed to get back to the b&b in Malham, so we made our excuses and left, driving past the tents bobbing in the flooded campsite to the Golden Lion. We were grateful that Jerome had come and although we were sorry the weather had let him down, our spirits were much improved for the rest of the walk. We wished him well, as he would be up early to get to his office in the morning. In the gloom we waved him off and ran back to the bunkhouse before the rain washed us away.

There was always the possibility that another person, or indeed a group of thirteen people could have arrived in the meantime and be snoring, farting and generally turning the woody bunkhouse into a midden. We thoughtlessly had not cleared up our sprawl of wet clothing and so we were relieved when we opened the door to see that the other bunks remained unoccupied.

We crawled into our sleeping bags. The rough wooden pine beds creaked and the plastic mattresses rustled as we tossed and turned. Outside the wind howled and the rain beat relentlessly against the Velux window.

## Farewell to Jerome

# FLASHBACK

**August 24, 1979**

In the Crown Inn at Horton-in-Ribblesdale the groups of people walking the Pennine Way stood with glass in hand and surreptitiously inspected each other. Sitting around one particular table was a gang of six walkers that we had not encountered before. They had their noses in their Wainwrights and were feverishly studying in preparation for the day ahead. This was puzzling because the next day was a very straightforward route with an obvious terminus at Hawes.

In the morning we saw them again at the edge of the campsite shoving their backpacks into a red Bedford van.

We were green with envy as we trudged by.

View from the ridge of Pen-y-Ghent

Mapping:
https://www.wikiloc.com/hiking-trails/pw-7-horton-in-ribblesdale-hawes-40883498

Ribblehead Viaduct

# Chapter 10 - Horton-in-Ribblesdale to Hawes

Total ascent: 12940 ft    Total distance: 106.62 miles

September 4th

**Chris:** My main 1979 memory of Hawes, Day 7's destination, is of a cheese shop on the busy main street. I was hoping it would still be there and, best case scenario, operating a cheese by post scheme so I could send some cheese back home. Of course, Hawes is 'the capital of Wensleydale', but I was hoping to find some Swaledale cheese (well Swaledale's only just over the next hill from here). Mag and I used to get our Swaledale fix from Waitrose, who once upon a time carried cows' and sheeps' milk versions of this delicious cheese but seem recently to have, very inconsiderately in my view, dropped both. I wasn't anticipating too demanding a day, so imagined we'd be in Hawes before closing time.

The small town is right in the middle of the Yorkshire Dales National Park and the route to it, again from memory is a lovely moorland walk. Prior to leaving this time however I noted that Wainwright feels differently, describing a large section of the route as a 'dreary expanse of moorland'. Nevertheless it's a day I've been looking forward to: when I think of the Pennine Way, today's admittedly fairly remote terrain is what naturally comes to mind. That image though, from forty years ago is bathed in sunshine, and recent precedent and the weather forecast suggest that this time sunshine may be in short supply.

However, on waking up in 2019 in the Golden Lion's bunkhouse, after thanking the Pennine Way gods for ensuring that nobody else had checked in to share this limited space, we were cheered by what

appeared to be a bright day outside. Our stuff, which had been comprehensively soaked yesterday was spread out across the vacant bunks and thankfully had fairly successfully dried out, but probably as a result of that process a fairly unpleasant clamminess pervaded the space. As I threw open the door, chilly air entered and cheerful autumn sunshine slanted its way across one side of the room. Could we hope for a better day?

**Triple decker bunks in the Golden Lion. Now imagine it full**

Over breakfast we wondered how prepared Jerome, now gone, might have been for a demanding return to work: he'd scheduled a six o'clock start for a drive from Malham to Lancaster and then a train journey to Edinburgh. Following yesterday's exertions, I imagine he would have slept on the train, though possibly fitfully: in Scotland he was to learn the future of his and his colleagues' jobs, and was understandably anxious.

Breakfast was served in the pub's restaurant, an unusually large room considering that today there are just four tables occupied. The Golden Lion and the accommodation it provides is a regular start and finish point for many who undertake the Yorkshire Three Peaks walks. The nearby Pen-y-Ghent, which we successfully out-manoeuvred yesterday, is one of the three. Apparently each year around a quarter of a million people undertake the challenging twenty-four mile circular walk that takes in Pen-y-Ghent, Ingleborough and Whernside and this popularity explains why the restaurant is so large – at times it must have to accommodate the hordes of Three Peaks walkers.

This morning though we were joined by just three other couples. Like us, they were bemused by the behaviour of the serving lady who seemed to be operating a milk rationing scheme – just one small sharing jug was available which had to be be moved from table to table as cereals and coffee were consumed. One middle aged chap was with his apparently teenage son who had mannerisms very similar to those of my own son Tom, and I thought I recognised the behaviour of a person who, like Tom, is on the autism spectrum. A little pang of homesickness stung me and I suddenly missed Tom: I'd love it if walking was something that appealed to him. It would be great to be on this trek with my son.

The milk shortage notwithstanding, yet another excellent full English was served up and thoroughly enjoyed: I speak for myself here though Duncan was showing no sign of wilting under this culinary onslaught.

Replete, and following what seemed to be becoming a regular pattern, the two of us only slowly prepared ourselves for the coming day. Our peers were up and gone long before us: Robin particularly prefers the early part of the day and was probably several miles ahead of us. We were in no hurry. The walk to Hawes is just over fourteen miles and we didn't expect it to be massively taxing.

Eventually packed and ready to leave, on stepping outside we were greeted by now startlingly bright sunshine, dazzling off the wet roads and roofs of the village. We'd been so disappointed by the weather to this point that I took a photo of the sunny sky on my phone and sent it home captioning it 'There's this weird round yellow thing in the sky…'. At about 9.45 we headed off north through the surprisingly deserted village leaving the road in front of the Crown Hotel, where we'd been fed gargantuan portions of curry and liver casserole the night before. When I was scheduling the walk, the plan had been to camp in Horton as we had forty years ago, but back then we were carrying food and would cook breakfast on the small portable stove. As we'd decided not to do that, planning involved finding somewhere to have breakfast on days when we had just vacated the tents. The Crown was very helpful in saying they would indeed provide us with breakfast despite our non-resident status, not needed as it turned out.

So this was Day 7 and it seemed somehow different. There were just the two of us again. It felt to me that now this was it, our new normal, just the two of us and the hills for probably – hopefully – another ten days. In the previous six days there seemed to have been so much to occupy our minds - just the novelty of being away, the uncertainty of whether to continue after the bereavement, Jerome joining us on the last three of those days - that I at least hadn't really felt the separateness from normal life that might have been expected. Now I did, and the superb scenery of the Dales helped cement the feeling as we climbed steadily but fairly quickly from seven hundred and fifty to twelve hundred feet.

This section of the Way is in the Yorkshire Dales National Park, a very popular walking area. The paths are good, often following old

**The gathering storm. The viaduct would soon disappear**

packhorse routes and generally broad enough to allow walking two abreast. They are clearly much used and are easily identified, being well signposted and maintained.

This early part of the day's route is shared with the Ribble Way, but that path branches off to the west after a couple of miles and heads in the general direction of Ribblehead. Way off in the distance we could just make out the arches of the famous viaduct. We took photographs that could hardly do it justice from so far away but the darkening clouds above it which were heading our way told us that they were the only photographs we'd get – it was obvious that we'd soon be unable to see anything like that far.

The path stays at twelve hundred feet for a couple of miles: it's easy and very enjoyable walking. As we walked, the fantastic views to the west kept coming but with some apprehension we watched the clouds building and being transported our way by the ever present strong wind.

Dipping down to Ling Gill Beck we spent a few minutes taking photographs. We commented on the remarkable brown-ness of the water rushing beneath the stone bridge spanning the beck, before starting the day's main climb, which would eventually attain eighteen hundred feet.

**Ling Gill Beck**

Somewhere on this climb the rain started, the cloud closed in and once again we were getting thoroughly wet.

**Looking back to Pen-y-Ghent before it too disappears into the gloom**

**Cloud, closing in**

For a while, as we traversed below the peak of Dodd Fell we were joined by an unusually tall dry stone wall which for a couple of miles provided tremendous shelter from the wind and horizontal stair rods that we would otherwise have had to endure. Eventually though this magnificent structure petered out and we were again at the mercy of the elements. The wind was so strong from our left that we had to lean sideways into it to have any hope of keeping upright, leaning over so far indeed that on the odd occasion when the wind momentarily dropped it was hard not to fall over.

Once again we were completely soaked in short order. Perhaps it was a day like this when Wainwright characterised it as dreary. Certainly the visibility was such that what should be a vista down the steep drop to Snaizeholme Beck, the similarly named Fell opposite and later into Widdale was non-existent.

Walking in these conditions is not conducive to conversation so inevitably my mind drifted away to other things. I had of course been keeping in frequent touch with Mag whose sister was still with her. One of her brothers was expected to arrive the following day, and they were hoping that the other sister might join them too, so they would be almost complete. Together they were working through all of the necessary tasks that follow a death, and were all grateful for the sharing of the burden. I imagined that the crunch for Mag would come after they had returned to their normal lives, likely to be a few days before I arrive home, and made a mental note to remain alert to any changes in her mood during that time. The funeral had been fixed for the week after that: at the moment there was no barrier to me continuing the walk.

The torrential rain and gale force wind continued as we passed alongside Dodd Fell and I was forced to search again for the 'I'm wet now but I'll be dry later' mindset from Day 3, but it was also becoming cold, making the wet harder to put up with. However, at

**The descent to Hawes, on a more pleasant day in 1979**

eleven and a half miles, we started to head downwards while turning slightly eastwards and almost immediately started to feel the benefit of some shelter from the higher ground we were leaving behind. The rain continued but with respite from the wind it felt less unpleasant as we lost height fairly rapidly on the approach to the village of Gayle, less than a mile from the centre of Hawes.

As we found our conversation muscles again, talk turned to where we might stay. Forty years ago we camped and the plan was to do the same this time but we fairly quickly and unanimously decided to seek b&b accommodation once we were in the town. I actually can't remember where we camped the first time, and the only campsite thrown up by my research this time was a disappointing mile or so from the town centre, so it wasn't a popular choice anyway. I'd checked the YHA in Hawes too and again, found it to be fully booked for this day.

Booked up by people like Robin and Simon in fact, both of whom we met on the main street of Hawes almost as soon as we arrived there. After a brief chat and a suggestion that we might see them later in one pub or another we headed off to find our own place to stay.

The rain had actually stopped and sunshine illuminated us as we entered the Crown, a pub on the high street. We ordered a drink and took advantage of the opportunity to begin the drying process. We didn't get too far with that though: a quick google and one phone call later we had a twin room booked at Cockett's, a small hotel which turned out to be literally next door. We drank up and relocated, and within minutes were being shown to our comfortable, though not huge room.

Showered and warmed and with still the best part of an hour of shopping time, Duncan went off in search of an extra garment. He too had been cold today and as there was no indication that climatically things might improve he wanted to feel more prepared. For me though, cheese was top of the shopping list. A quick but disappointing recce of the main shopping street failed to locate any cheese shop that fitted the memory I had brought with me, so I followed the signs to the Wensleydale Creamery, a few minutes' walk from the town centre. This is not just a shop but a whole visitor centre, production site, education centre, museum and lunch venue. Alas what it isn't is a purveyor of any form of Swaledale.

The putative sixty years plus Pennine Way walker reading this might be wondering about now, a week in, how we were coping with the demands of the walk. My sense was that Duncan and I were in pretty much the same place physically; basically we were doing just fine. I had had no knee trouble at all since Hebden Bridge and I don't think either of us were finding the walking too great a challenge. Some of the walks we'd had in places like the Sierra Nevada were far more demanding than anything the Pennines had thrown at us so far. We've also walked in blazing heat, (Spain again), in the horrible, cold wet conditions of a Slovakian spring, the still snow clad mountains of the Picos in northern Spain and on the ridiculously steep paths of the Vikos Gorge in northern Greece and always coped well. Logically then, we were able to argue that we should definitely be capable of completing the Pennine Way.

What we couldn't be sure of is how we'd cope with the demands being placed upon us day after day after day, without break but so far I was happy with how things were going. That isn't to say that at the end of each day we weren't tired. After a meal and a couple of pints – and perhaps a whisky – we were definitely ready for sleep by about ten o'clock.

Forty years ago, after a couple of days' acclimatisation to the daily walking, we began to feel stronger and stronger and all things considered I felt just as strong as that now. I was very confident that we could complete the walk, barring unforeseen injury or illness.

We spent the evening in the pub next door where we had the opportunity for the first time to chat at length with Robin, the intrepid walker from the US. Explaining that this was our second time on the Pennine Way, we were able to enthuse about the following day's walk out of Wensleydale into Swaledale, definitely one of my favourite days. We retired looking forward to a day filled with wonderful scenery and which unusually for a Pennine Way day, would end high up - at Tan Hill - where of course we'd find England's highest pub.

Stone houses, Hawes, 1979

Mapping:
https://www.wikiloc.com/hiking-trails/pw-8-hawes-to-tan-hill-40388511

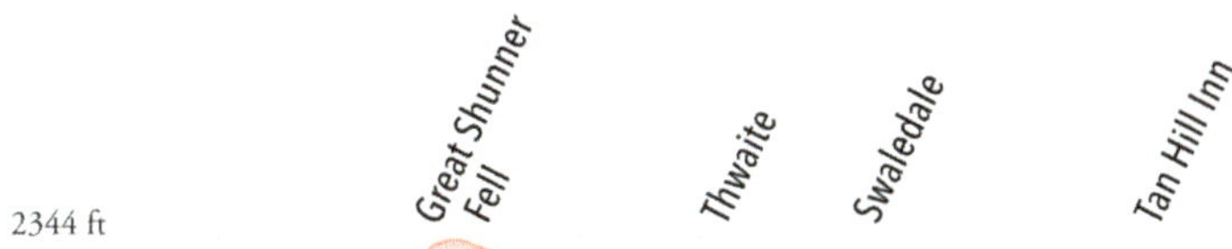


2344 ft

# Chapter 11 - Hawes to Tan Hill

734 ft 16.26 mi

Total ascent: 15867 ft Total distance: 122.88 miles

September 5th

**Duncan:** For the morning to arrive and to actually be woken by daylight was a first for me on this journey. It was a relief to enjoy a full night of sleep. We turned on the television to catch the weather forecast and avoid any news of Brexit. Which was impossible, especially as the media have a new word, whose meaning just a few days previously would have floored even the most gifted lexicographer. Now, to prorogue, proroguing and prorogation were on everyone's lips as it became the hottest of hot topics.

Speaking of hot topics, I put on the new base layer I bought yesterday from the country shop in Hawes in the hope that today I might experience warmth. The last seven days of walking had taught me that I'd made a huge mistake in removing the fleece from my backpack just before the off.

My garments in the drying room were satisfyingly clean and dry and only my boots were still damp. Rob had commented after coming over Pen-y-Ghent that when it comes to the Pennine Way, no amount of Gore-Tex can keep the wet at bay and this was becoming a self-evident truth.

The serving lady in the restaurant was as bright and cheerful as the sunlight flooding in through the high windows as she flitted between the tables, taking orders and bringing food. The breakfast (full English of course) was lovely and we gladly paid and left.

**Opposite: a pleasant stroll beside the River Ure**

Outside, the sun was reflecting off the wet tarmac. We crossed the high street to stock up on lunch items from the Spar shop. The deli counter enticed us with a wonderful selection of home made black puddings and it was sad to have to leave such a delicacy behind. Our packs were now filled with sandwiches, pork pies, scotch eggs and fruit as we left the capital of the Dales and headed north.

Hardraw was reached after a pleasant stroll starting beside the River Ure which meandered through strikingly green pasture where sheep grazed on high quality grass that looked much more palatable than the scraggy sedges of the moors. A roller and fork had been left in the middle of the cricket pitch and it was all starting to look and feel like a typical English summer day.

**Typically English**

The Green Dragon Inn stands guard over the entrance to Hardraw Force, England's highest waterfall, contained within its own magnificent rocky amphitheatre. We took a look forty years ago and don't feel the need today.

We pass the bunkhouse, which was Rob's resting place for the previous evening and think that it's sad that we won't see him again as he accelerates up the Pennine Way.

Ahead of us was the massive hump of Great Shunner Fell. It is five miles of continuous ascent and I have memories of it being fairly arduous, mainly because the route is a long series of false summits.

Our younger selves found the uphill walk tiring that day, so we halted to brew up some coffee. Today in a sheltered hollow about two-

**Hardraw Force in '79,**
**there are people behind the waterfall**

thirds of the way up we stumbled across the Father and Son doing the same, probably in the same hollow. The son, a tall, thin man with a mop of dark brown hair was taking in the view while languidly smoking a cigarette. A rare sight amongst modern walkers. Meanwhile the father tended the burner.

We stopped and chatted for a moment as they were both cheery souls, despite or maybe because of the task they have set themselves. It turns out they were not aiming to complete the journey to John O'Groats in one trip but will stop at Keld, which we will pass today and return next year, batteries recharged and with a new intermediate target to be achieved. They were a remarkable pair.

We headed uphill to the sprawling summit which we attained in just over two hours from Hawes. For the first time since we began this walk we have comprehensively beaten our younger selves as the record shows that they took two and half hours to get to the summit cairn (although to be fair, those youngsters did make and drink a cup of coffee on the way).

**The sprawling summit of Great Shunner Fell**

We had reached a viewpoint par excellence as this is the highest point of the walk so far. Ahead of us was the beautiful green valley of Swaledale, looking back we could see Pen-y-Ghent and to our west on the far horizon were the sharp peaks of Lakeland.

**On top of Great Shunner Fell but not on top of this selfie thing...**

There was something missing in these expansive views. Something that was ever present in the other wild places that we have walked in Europe and that's the constant surveillance of large birds of prey. The raptors that top the food chain, that dive and swoop for small mammals or slowly circle in thermals surveying the ground for carrion were an extremely rare sight on the heights of the Pennines.

There are a variety of reasons for this, all disputed by the various parties involved but the simple fact is that the Pennine hilltops no longer resemble the original wilderness that covered Britain in the past. Thousands of years ago, most of the land up to a height of sixteen hundred feet was covered in forest. Man cleared it away.

Some claim that the moorland that covers the tops of the Pennines is almost as intensively farmed as a battery chicken shed because everything is geared to producing the maximum number of game birds for the late summer and autumnal shoots. The management regime of the moors includes burning heather to produce new growth for fattening the grouse, increasing the drainage and cutting roads into the moor to ease access for the shooters. All this is proven to be doing lasting damage to the blanket bog. At the same time vermin are ruthlessly culled including it is suggested, birds of prey, which are accused of taking young grouse chicks, thereby reducing the abundance of these stupid birds that squawk loudly when disturbed and have all the airborne manoeuvrability of a canal boat in flight.

Hundreds and thousands of grouse are shot on the moors and I imagined that their final destination is on the menu of the finest restaurants. However, in restaurant kitchens, game birds are disliked mainly because they are so difficult to pluck. The birds don't come ready prepared and of course there may still be some shot in them. There is little meat and one bird adds up to a serving. Most recipes involve a large amount of red wine and garlic as grouse on its own has a fairly uninspiring taste. Even then grouse is not a popular choice with the dining public.

So if it isn't eaten what happens to all the grouse meat? It seems a small percentage goes abroad but in this country there is little demand for it so most of it ends up in pet food and agricultural products.

People who disagree with grouse shooting are often characterised as vegan weirdos or townies with no knowledge of the workings of the countryside. There is very little common ground between those who like to shoot things and those who don't. My personal preference would be that shooting should be for a reason: for example most of the farmers where we walk in Essex would be glad to welcome people to shoot the pigeons during planting time.

Between the entrenched battle lines there are those who are seeking a more nuanced solution. Simulated grouse shooting, which is essentially clay pigeon shooting on the high moors is one such suggestion. This has been successfully trialed and has several advantages over the traditional shoot in that it is an activity that can carry on all year round, rather than merely during the season. A major benefit of removing the seasonal aspect is the possibility of increasing full time employment opportunities.

Simulated grouse shooting is also a sport without blood, and the side activities of heather burning and vermin control are rendered unnecessary, allowing regeneration of the moors. If this is the future then maybe the skies will be filled once more with the soaring flight of large birds of prey, like they are in Essex where the buzzard and red kite have become a common sight. I personally believe this would be an outcome that all lovers of the countryside would find inspiring.

Looking around at the view, we were feeling good and although the wind was still with us, the weather was generally just a gnat's better. Standing on the summit of Great Shunner we checked out the weather forecast for the evening. A deep trough carrying heavy rain was scheduled to sit over Tan Hill for the whole night and as a consequence we had no problem agreeing to book a room, even though it was the most expensive accommodation of the trip so far.

Having sorted out the issue of where we were sleeping, the downhill walk became a pleasant stroll. To our right we could see the rural beauty of Swaledale, the ribbon of water in the valley, set amongst green fields lined with dry stone walls and dotted with lonely barns. Ahead of us was the picture perfect village of Thwaite.

**How can you get lost in a one street village?**

We entered the village at about a quarter to two and we were surprised to find a little cafe nestling in the sunshine, serving teas. We walked on but misread the map and headed up the road towards Richmond. Quickly, Wikiloc warned us that we'd left the path and we corrected our error and turned back to pass the tea shop once more. Wikiloc had warned us many times, mainly to alert us that the actual route of the Pennine Way had subtly altered from the archival OS Map. This was one of the very few occasions when we actually went the wrong way.

By now the Father and Son partnership were settling in to the cafe for some well earned lunch, something that we would have considered doing if we weren't already carrying it.

On the path up the other side of the valley we found a comfortable place to sit and eat as we enjoyed the view along Swaledale across to Muker. Although it felt as though we'd come a long way, it was still

seven miles to Tan Hill with a lot more uphill before we finish this evening. The clouds rolled in and with them came gentle showers. We donned our wet weather gear, pulled the rain covers over our sacks and climbed to the high daleside path.

The view was stunning. Upper Swaledale is one of the most beautiful places in Britain and this path between Thwaite and Keld has remarkable views across it. For three miles, it was an utter delight for the eyes.

My boots had a very different view of the terrain. On crossing Great Shunner Fell we also left the limestone country that we first met in Malham and this path was a regression to more agricultural mud. My grip on the ground was non-existent and I was slipping and sliding dangerously. It was genuinely worrying how little traction I had and it

**The stunning Upper Swaledale**

caused me to do the splits, not something I considered possible at my age. If the walking equivalent of an Ofsted inspector was appraising my style the final assessment would have read 'Flailing'.

Sadly I had to ignore the outstanding views around me and concentrated fully on the path. Each step was carefully considered and countermeasures taken when the unexpected occurred. Although we were progressing quite slowly, the Father and Son had almost come to a halt. We passed them for the last time a half a mile before Keld, wishing them well in their quest.

The Pennine Way does not enter Keld and instead heads down to cross the Swale beside East Gill Force, a confluence of pretty waterfalls where a tributary joins the Swale. Glimpsed through the trees in a sunlit glade above us, a couple were engaged in a romantic liaison. We ignored them as we stopped for a while to enjoy the view back down the valley.

I slipped my water bottle out of the side pocket and headed to a vantage point to savour the spectacle of the falls while sipping some water, knowing that this would be my last chance to see any part of Swaledale. Chris wandered past me with his water bottle in hand. I turned back to where we'd left the backpacks to sort out my rain

cover. A few moments later Chris returned with a deeply worried look and his brow is bruised and bloody.

'Did you see what happened?'

No, I had not.

**Chris:** A few yards from where we'd settled for a short break, a feeder stream was crashing through trees and rocks down the steep drop to the Swale. Swollen by recent rainfall, the raging torrent seemed to provide the perfect opportunity to replenish my water supply. I left Duncan relaxing and headed across the large, perfectly flat rocks that resembled a giant staircase bordering the water. As I approached I realised that the benign looking surface was slippier than any ice rink. Suddenly my feet were going in all directions. I was unable to avoid falling and hit my hip painfully on a sharp rock. Struggling to my feet, trying to get a grip on the rock rising to my left while also holding on to the water bottle, I managed a step or two more before in a repeat performance I hit the deck again, this time hitting my forehead. Simultaneously, as my arm flailed in a vain attempt to retain balance, the bottle left my hand and flew off into the air. I needed a few

**The beguiling but dangerous East Gill Force**

seconds to gather myself. I looked around, hoping to find the water bottle and spotted it, by bizarre good fortune, jammed upright in rocks in the stream, gradually filling itself. I was just able to reach it, screwed the top on and turned to make my way back to safety, opting now not to even attempt to stand, but sliding along on my rear end.

Back with Duncan I described what must have been a comical looking episode, but I realised I had actually been very lucky. It was pure chance that I'd slipped in the direction I had - if I'd gone the other way I'd have joined the river in a headlong dash many feet into the valley bottom. It would probably have been the end of the Way for me and the bloody forehead reminded me of the need for care and concentration.

**Duncan:** While this mayhem had been taking place about fifty yards away on the main path the canoodling couple were now engaged in what could only be described as strenuous courtship. Although clothing had yet to be discarded, it was surely only a matter of time before the raging hormones on show were going to, er, have their day. They were actually situated bang on the path (which was an accurate description both of their location and where this was all leading) and we had no choice but to walk closely by, not that they seemed to be aware of our presence at all.

The last four miles to Tan Hill were on muddy farmland which quickly changed to open moorland before reverting to the inevitable bog. Flagstones were nowhere to be seen and although the sun was still shining it was wet underfoot. The last time we came this way we retreated to the road as the bog was very bad, but this time we stuck to the path.

Above us on the horizon there was a lone house. It was Tan Hill Inn, England's highest inn: warmth, hot showers and beer. Life doesn't get better than this. Or more expensive, as Tan Hill has a monopoly on accommodation hereabouts. We could have put the tent up as the weather was deceptively pleasant at the moment but there's no chance of that as we headed to our room. This was quite the tightest fit of any

**That's boggin', best said in a strong Glaswegian accent**

place so far, with barely enough space to open the door, let alone negotiate our two large backpacks. On the wall was a picture of Brenda Blethyn playing the role of television detective Vera Stanhope. She is entering the main bar with her assistant in an episode that it turned out was broadcast later in the year. This was one of many publicity pictures that were around the Inn including a captioned picture of 'Python' Griff Rhys Jones, which must be news to him and the surviving Pythons. Returning downstairs after washing and unpacking we saw Simon and Robin eating together in the Lounge Bar and they gestured for us to join them. When we entered the bar earlier the owners had suggested that we should book for dinner, as if we might be tempted to pop out and check on the local restaurant scene. The booking, it transpired was for a small dining room at the back of the Inn but we would rather stay here and converse. That was until we discovered that Simon had taken on the role of *Keeper of the Rules of the Pennine Way*. He had spied us heading off up the road at Thwaite earlier and was about to conclude, until we returned to the path, that we were 'cheating' again. This did not prevent him from suggesting it.

I've read quite a lot about walking and nowhere have I come across an actual rule book. There is a lot of guidance but no significant structure, which to me is one of the appealing aspects of the pastime. Once rules become involved the next step is competition and at that moment I start to lose interest in the whole thing.

However Simon was just getting into his stride. In his mind the Pennine Way was a sacred track whose course must be followed to the step. We pointed out that on the first day, we ignored the official route to follow in the footsteps of our younger selves. We did the 'vintage' route if you will, or indeed the 'authentic' one, we could argue. And anyway, we have done it all before, so we were not concerned about the route taken.

If there are any rules, they are personal and not something that others can use against me. I guess that mine would simply state that I have to walk all the way. Which way is very much up to me. The many guidebooks do offer alternative routes and if I were to decide that I would rather visit some other place, then that would become my personal Pennine Way. Even the old curmudgeon Wainwright used to encourage a little detour here and there.

In reality I was not interested in Simon's debate. My mind wandered and I suddenly become aware of the deep black darkness outside. At the same time a younger couple entered the inn. In the hierarchy of walking gear, their's definitely looked the highest spec so far. They settled in a warm corner and consulted guide books which betrayed that they were walking the Way.

Meanwhile a minstrel had started playing tunelessly in the main bar. The mildly discordant music drifted through to the lounge and seemed to be the cue for people to leave.

**Thwaite post box in 1979 (above) and 2019 (below)**

## FLASHBACK

**August 26, 1979**

At Tan Hill Inn the same core group of walkers arrived and quietly acknowledged each other. Some were quite chatty, especially a suburban couple from Brum that we had met several times along the Way, who would cheerfully mingle amongst the groups that they considered to be more hardened walkers with their sing-song catch phrase 'Keeping up with three-weekers'.

A lot of the talk among the group was about a man who had died the previous week on Sleightholme Moor, whose brooding presence could be viewed to the north-east from the Inn. Across this deadly moor two figures in brightly coloured cagoules could be seen careering across the bog. They arrived just as dusk was setting in and cast their tent. People crowded around them, eager for news of the state of the path. They were walking north to south at a heroic rate of over forty miles a day, with the intention of finishing within a week.

The group of six that we had named 'Wainwrights out' had hogged a corner in the bar to continue their incessant evening planning sessions. However, we noticed something strange. The driver of their van was not the same person, it changed every day. This revealing fact did not encompass the spirit of the Pennine Way, we felt.

(Am I being judgemental here? In which case I plead guilty to hypocrisy. )

**Opposite: Tan Hill Inn where, as Webster's beers announced you could 'Drink the Pennine Way.'**

Tan Hill Inn
ENGLAND'S HIGHEST INN 1732'' A.S.L.
WEBSTER'S BEERS
DRINK THE PENNINE WAY
WEBSTER'S BEERS

Mapping:
https://www.wikiloc.com/hiking-trails/pw-9-tan-hill-to-middleton-in-teesdale-40388520

## A miscellany of faecal matter as found on Sleightholme Moor

*With apologies to the Bristol Stool Scale*

**Type 1:** Unavoidable, common, persistent

**Type 2:** Firm, lumpy.
nb. could just be grouse feed.

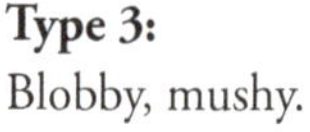

**Type 3:**
Blobby, mushy.

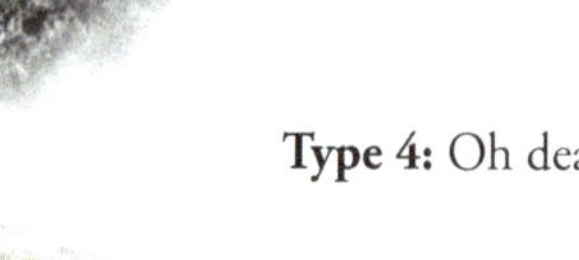

**Type 4:** Oh dear.

**Type 5:** *Megaturdus occulta*. You didn't step in that did you?

1723 ft

# Chapter 12 - Tan Hill to Middleton-in-Teesdale

716 ft 16.36 mi

Total ascent: 17163 ft Total distance: 139.24 miles

September 6th

**Chris**: I remember well waking up on 27th August 1979: the ground we'd pitched the tent on was extremely hard and we'd had considerable difficulty finding a rockless patch big enough to accommodate us. On 6th September 2019 I awoke in a comfortable warm bed in a first floor room. I was pleased that on our arrival at the Tan Hill Inn we'd availed ourselves of its b&b facilities as the 'campsite' had looked pretty much the same yesterday afternoon as it did forty years ago, except wetter.

I remember too on that day forty years ago looking across the infamous Sleightholme Moor immediately to the north of the Inn to where the early morning sun was glinting off the windows of cars passing on the busy A66, some three miles to the north. There was no chance of enjoying such a vista this time: as we consumed another cooked breakfast we watched through the windows as the weather, which hadn't been good when we first looked, deteriorated rapidly. Those horizontal stair rods were there again and nothing was visible beyond the end of the car park. Agreeing that the conditions were seriously uninviting, we decided to hang about and see if things

**Well would you go out in it?**

improved. We watched on as Simon, with whom we'd had breakfast, packed himself up and headed into the maelstrom.

The 'infamy' of Sleightholme Moor originates in the fact that it is essentially a bog. We heard on our first visit that lives had been lost out there on the moor, and tales of people going in 'up to their waist'. To be fair 1979 was a relatively dry year but I don't recall Duncan and I having much trouble; I do remember us discussing our joint view that if you are careful and look where you are putting your feet, disaster is readily averted. The trick I think is to step on the densest tussocks that are within reach and don't step in water. This time too I found it quite bearable. The truth is that it isn't actually very far, probably little more than a couple of miles from where the bogginess starts to where the path meets Sleightholme Beck and becomes good again.

One blogger describes Sleightholme as 'a bleak puddle of sopping misery that can go f**k itself'. Perhaps a rather extreme reaction, or

**Heading onto Sleightholme, perhaps to our deaths...**

maybe just one that reflects a difference in conditions between April (when he did it) and September. Nevertheless, the moor is one part of the Pennine Way where slabs would have been a pleasing innovation.

I was pleased to see that as we crossed Sleightholme the conditions were not enough to dull Duncan's creative spirit. Somewhere here he was inspired to start the photographic chronicling of the almost infinite variety of faecal matter to be found on the moors, in the manner of the Bristol Stool Chart. It could be his magnum opus, his masterpiece.

Soon after, the crossing of the A66 marks the half way point of the Pennine Way. Whilst I accept this piece of information as fact, it is hard to process, because this place feels so 'up north' to me. In my teenage years my brother lived in Carlisle and my parents and I usually travelled there via the A66. We'd often stop to eat a sandwich around here and I remember a sense of the remoteness of the place and a feeling of being at the top end of England. The realisation –

**Wet, but we've encountered worse**

reminder really – that there's a lot more of 'the north' to come hits me in a rather daunting way: we've completed a hundred and thirty-five miles but there's still the same to walk, but in less time. There will be longer, and very possibly harder days ahead.

Those picnic lunches would have been eaten in a lay-by on what was then a single carriageway road which the Pennine Way walker would have crossed. Today, the A66 is a busy dual carriageway, but we hardly noticed the road or its traffic as we were directed through a tunnel that now takes walkers beneath it.

By now the early rain had cleared and we walked on, revelling in what finally appeared to be lasting sunshine, though the occasional cloud did get in the way. My recall of walking here is no more than a feeling, one of pleasant walking in peaceful, gently rolling if unspectacular countryside with virtually no sign of habitation, on a lovely sunny day. Wainwright calls most of the walking from Tan Hill to Middleton 'second rate' but again I'd take issue with him: nobody could deny that this panorama is extremely attractive.

The experience this time matches the first time, except we are still beset by a stiff wind and are always half expecting rain to return. Heading just slightly west of due north, the path crosses the undulations that run east-west, dropping down into the valleys of Baldersdale and Lunedale, flooded in parts to create numerous reservoirs that provide a water supply to Teeside. Considering the amount of rain there has been we were surprised to see the water levels

*Chapter Twelve*

# Second rate some say, but I like it

in the reservoirs so low, revealing a small stone bridge over what was once the course of the river Lune.

The biggest climb of the day, something like five hundred feet over a couple of miles came as a bit of a shock after the gentler slopes of the morning, the kind of ascent that stops any pretence of conversation. It took us out of Lunedale to a point where the path turns north east and Teesdale is revealed for the first time. Our destination, the small town of Middleton-in-Teesdale, lies seemingly scattered around the

bottom of a broad, shallow basin through which the River Tees passes.

The Pennine Way-er taking in this excellent vista can see beyond the town to where the following day's exciting walking will take them. We could also see mountainous clouds building to our left and though it wasn't raining on us at that moment it clearly was somewhere: as we started the descent to Middleton a magnificent rainbow appeared

**The old bridge over the River Lune**

ahead of us, a complete, bright arc spanning the whole of the valley directly over the town and seeming to come to earth a few fields ahead. It was a quite remarkable sight and the panorama functions on both our cameras were put to the test over the next ten or fifteen minutes as the rainbow persisted.

As we completed the descent to the bridge over the Tees that marks the entry to the town, once again the question of the night's accommodation was broached. As on earlier nights, my schedule would have had us heading to the local campsite but as the alert reader will have gathered by now, we were no longer in the market for that sort of thing. Besides, we were fairly sure we'd have no option but to camp the next night at Dufton, so a decision was made to call up

some local b&b's. From a convenient bench in Horsemarket, part of the main road through the town, we set about googling, hoping for the best. Again, within a couple of minutes a twin room was secured, and we were walking the last quarter mile of the day to the very comfortable Teesdale Hotel. A warm welcome awaited us there and we were soon settled into our room, relaxing and looking forward to an evening in the hotel's restaurant and bar.

While Duncan made the most of the bath that the hotel had thoughtfully provided, I went out in the street to find a signal and

**The rainbow directly over Middleton-in-Teesdale**

made a call home. I was pleased to find that Mag still seemed to be doing well, the siblings were still around and were enjoying their time together.

Around seven we repaired to the bar of the hotel: we were pretty tired and opted not to scour the small town for the most exciting Friday night opportunities it might have to offer. Besides, the menu was an interesting one, offering several rarely seen dishes even in a gastropub with clear fine dining leanings. It was definitely the first time I'd had 'ultimate' kedgeree in a pub and though my excited anticipation was dulled by the arrival of a sub-optimally sized portion, this culinary eclecticism sparked reminiscences of the food we enjoyed the first time.

Our food then had literally been a moveable feast. Well, mobile anyway, and to be honest, not exactly a feast. Dried foods that we'd brought with us and tinned foods that were picked up in shops along the way and which could be prepared on a single gas burner, provided breakfast on camping days. Evening meals, whenever it was possible (mostly) were taken in a pub, usually to be found fairly close to wherever we happened to be staying overnight. Pubs were far more easily found even in smaller villages then than they are now: the sad decline of pub numbers particularly in recent years has meant that day walks with a pub lunch must now be carefully researched to ensure that firstly there is a pub en route and then that it actually opens at lunchtime.

The concept of the gastropub wasn't even a twinkle in some marketing person's eye forty years ago and to say that pub food was (generally) fairly uninteresting is probably doing the chefs a favour. We dined frequently on a piece of browny grey stuff which seemed to be available everywhere and appeared on the menu as the Dalesteak, a probably frozen, factory produced 'meat' pattie that was exactly the same pretty well wherever we landed – served with chips and peas of course. One night, in Bellingham I think, we were so ravenously hungry that we ate this dinner twice! My guess is though that it was fairly cheap – an important aspect of dining out in those days when we were lowly NHS workers. Had there been more up market options available we probably wouldn't have been able to afford them.

While we waited to be fed our chat was interrupted by a remarkably raucous bunch of revellers who invaded the bar for a pre-prandial, before thankfully clearing off to the restaurant. Now I like a bit of life in a pub but what a bleedin' racket! We suspected that these were the very same shooters we had encountered earlier in the day on Harter's Fell, a few miles short of Middleton, but now with their women folk in tow. If one thing had broken the peace and quiet of the day's walk it had been the occasional report of grouse shooters' guns which became louder as we neared Middleton. We had said hello to a little gang of them gathered around their 4x4s and were surprised that there hadn't been any warning anywhere about the possibility of this stuff going on. Can you just go shooting on land that a national trail is passing through without mentioning you're doing it?

Eventually returning to non-shouted conversation after the shooters were called to their table, we enjoyed a whisky and struck up conversation with a group of three late comers, one very effusive and inquisitive about our experience so far, and his two quieter mates.

The chatty one it seemed ran some sort of outward bound company that would among other things transfer your kit from stop to stop along the Way. He had dragged his buddies out for a weekend of 'research'. Intending to find out what the hills and walking were all about, they'd established base camp at Langdon Beck YHA, seven or eight miles further north along the Way from Middleton. The hostel is a popular staging post for Pennine Way-ers, but I'm glad that both times we've passed this way we've stayed in Middleton: the following day's walk heads straight into the wonderful Tees valley, a beautiful and occasionally spectacular walk that deserves to be enjoyed when fresh, not at the end of the day when all you are thinking about is getting the pack off and having a rest. We recommended to the trio that they should, like us, go to Dufton for their walk the following day: we knew exactly what excitement that walk had to offer and suggested that they definitely shouldn't miss it. As we wandered off to our room, we were looking forward to High Cup already.

# *Chapter Twelve*

**The cattle market, Middleton-in-Teesdale 1979**

Mapping:
https://www.wikiloc.com/hiking-trails/pw-10-middleton-in-teesdale-to-dufton-40388529

Nichol Chair, High Cup in 1979

# Chapter 13 - Middleton-in-Teesdale to Dufton

Total ascent: 18958 ft
Total distance: 159.08 miles

September 7th

**Duncan:** We were sitting in the wood panelled dining room of the Teesdale Hotel awaiting our sixth consecutive daily cooked breakfast. The hotel had seen better days and though the decor was tired, the whole place had more charm than the entire catalogue of Premier Inns and Travelodges put together.

The only other early morning guests were four people in a shooting party, part of the raucous bunch of revellers that had noisily invaded the bar the night before. Now they sported garish tweed trousers matched with waistcoats, or knitted sleeveless tops of prismatically challenging colour and pattern. A peacock display of clothing that spoke more of their wealth than their taste. This ostentatious spectacle was in marked contrast to their hushed conversation as they were nursing hangovers. As our platters arrived the party gathered their guns, all held in expensive leather covers. I suspected that last night's overindulgence had left them wholly unprepared for the day ahead as they staggered out to do battle with their prey, which I suppose gave the grouse a fighting chance.

I am reminded of a time many years earlier when I had arrived at a hotel in Dorset to film an interview with a doctor. There was a group of men in tweeds mustering by the front door as I entered with my tripod in its sling case. They must have thought I was carrying a gun as they politely inquired if I was joining their party. We talked at cross purposes for a few seconds before the penny dropped that I was there for a very different shoot. They departed a few moments later and I asked hotel manager if the party was shooting nearby, as that would make the audio on the recording somewhat challenging, with our interviewee's comments interspersed with gunfire. Fortunately (for us, not the game birds) they were being ferried to some far flung moor to engage the enemy.

We ate our breakfast and contemplated the day ahead. All along the Way so far local people had commented that 'tomorrow the weather will be better' and it never was but this sharply sunny morning was full of promise.

We tied up our boots on the benches beneath the imposing golden stone facade of the hotel. On the other side of the road was a butcher's shop where we stocked up with pork pies and biscuits, enough to fuel us to Dufton.

As we joined the mighty River Tees, the last of the thin high cloud gave way to full sunshine, the path was firm and dry and the river was flowing fast with all the recent rain, especially over the waterfalls of Low Force. Further upriver, canoeists manoeuvred amongst the rapids, weaving between the rocks and spinning through whirlpools. We stood and watched as they negotiated some of the smaller falls,

**Low Force and canoeists (opposite)**

twisting and splashing their way through the fast flowing brown water.

The path held onto the south side of the river passing the occasional footbridge. For a change, there were other walkers, not merely those who were walking the Way, families and day trippers and all were cheered by the warm sunshine.

A few hundred yards before High Force a viewpoint had been built just off the path. I don't think it was possible to see the waterfall from a distance forty years ago, or maybe we walked straight past the viewpoint in our eagerness to reach the falls. This grassy platform offered a fine view of the cascading water a quarter of mile upriver.

Beside High Force there was a small disinfectant station where we were required to clean our boots before moving on. Some years previously, the fungal infection *Phytophthora austrocedi* was found to be attacking the juniper woodland of Upper Teesdale. Left unchecked the results of this disease would be devastating for this extremely rare habitat and so this seemingly puny protection had been installed. It was now over eight years since this defence was deployed and the bushes that looked like gorse were in fact juniper, so the evidence suggested that it must be working.

# FLASHBACK

**August 28, 1979**

**Chris at High Force in full 'clothes-horse' mode**

After the first few days the groups of walkers along the Way proceeded in almost complete silence. Conversation was not merely exhausted, it had been flogged to death and all that was left was the transactional, the main triggers being route finding, nature spotting and eating. It was a glimpse into a meditative state of zen-like calm, unless this was gatecrashed by a lone walker who had examined the zen-like state and decided that you can't beat a bit of inane conversation. One such person appeared around the time we left Middleton-in-Teesdale. He flitted between the various groups and was as welcome as a wasp at a picnic. After engaging with a brief 'Good morning,' he would adjust his pace and long outstay the norms of polite walker conversation. We quickly learnt too much about him, for example that he travelled on days off to collect railway tickets from stations with unusual names. Snodland was one such mildly amusing place. It was the type of pastime that spoke of a crushed life behind a civil service desk.

It was a relief when he finally upped his pace and set his sights on one of the other groups.

People clambering over High Force

Forty years ago there were very few lone walkers, most of the people walking were either in pairs or groups. The solitary walker was a rare beast because the prevailing view was that in the case of emergency the risks were too high. What help could be summoned if you were injured or trapped? The mobile phone has ended that dilemma and the balance now favours solitary walkers over groups. It seemed that having set off alone they preferred to keep it that way, when they were walking at least.

## High Force

The River Tees was a delightful companion. Running in huge loops along a verdant valley, the clear brown water sparkled. The occasional angler swished a rod in the hope of hooking a hungry brown trout. Crossing the river at Cronkley Bridge we left Yorkshire for the last time and entered the County of Durham for a few glorious miles.

In quite a few places on the Pennine Way and especially along this section, the water leached through into small pools on the path and the surface shimmered with an oily rainbow. My first thought on seeing this phenomenon was that it was a sign of pollution.

**A sparkling loop of the River Tees**

**An oily film**

Fortunately, that is not the case because this tell-tale film commonly occurs where water has percolated through shale. There is a large amount of shale under the Pennine hills and some of it had been earmarked for fracking. Hopefully the moratorium on fracking holds and these most perfect of views are never sullied by industry.

At a curve of the river under Falcon Clints, the path was suddenly hemmed in and it became necessary to scramble, hop and stretch over scree and large rocks. The pace slowed as we focussed on the uneven ground. I placed my right foot on a rock in a deeper crevice and it held securely. I stepped forward with my left seeking the next safe place but the rock shifted and I couldn't find a secure footing. In slow motion I sank forward and because I was unable to do anything to prevent my gradual decline I ended up face down, sprawled across the boulders. I looked behind and Chris, oblivious to my fate, glanced up to find me spread eagled across the path. At last I was able to regain some semblance of control and I managed to pull my right foot free of the crevice. I was very fortunate that no damage was done (except to my pride) and we continued, with care.

Beyond Falcon Clints we came across the young couple we had seen at Tan Hill. They were enjoying lunch in the warm sunshine beside the river and brewing up tea on a stove. They asked us where we're staying tonight and we replied that we were putting our tents up in the campsite in Dufton. They will be there also and have booked a 'Hobbit Hole' which turned out to be accommodation a grade above a tent; a wooden hut, with heating and maybe a mattress where they can lay their sleeping bags. When all we had to look forward to was our tents, this sounded very enticing indeed.

The two hundred and sixty feet high cataracts of Cauldron Snout are the most spectacular water feature of the day. The roar could be heard before the falls came into sight. Just how much noise the brown river water makes is dependent on the flow regulated from Cow Green reservoir above. Today a torrent had been set free and the cataracts were letting rip.

Surprisingly, the green path beside the river which had led us to this point disappeared and a look up confirmed that some scrambling was going to be necessary to get to the top. In a short distance there was a lot of height to be gained and no particular route to be followed. This was a much bigger challenge than Grindsbrook Clough in that it was much more vertical. Although the actual climbing was very easy, my legs still didn't have any strength and I was unable to step up as I would have expected. Instead I had to use my knees to push me up. This huge exertion caused my muscles yet again to turn to jelly, a jarring repeat of the first day and I wondered how the enormous amount of exercise that had brought me to this point somehow had failed to increase my stamina.

I suppose that my physique tends more towards the 'Hugh Fearnley-Whittingstall' than 'He-man' and made a mental note that maybe I should make time for some straightforward exercise in future.

In retrospect I have come to the conclusion that the lack of power in my legs stems from the long-standing problem in my back. When my back was seizing up many years ago so were my legs. By the time I met the therapist with the Nordic Massager I was unable to run and sometimes even walking was difficult, which probably was my body's response to protect the bottom of my spine. Then, the muscles in my legs felt like rods of iron. The various machines that I use daily have slowly brought the muscles back from their frozen state. Each time a muscle is released it is quite dramatic because my body has to respond and relearn how to move. My theory now is that when I was faced with a severe climb, there were muscles that had not been exercised at all and therefore complained loudly when asked to work hard. Like here and on the first day in Grindsbrook.

Slowly and with a series of breaks we progressed up the side of the roaring cataracts. At the top, we settled down to regain our breath and eat some lunch. Apart from the last half hour, it'd been a steady eleven mile climb with still another five miles to come before the descent into Dufton, so a pork pie and a drink was much appreciated. Sitting

# *Chapter Thirteen*

**The roaring cataracts of Cauldron Snout**

in the sun and sheltered from the wind, we considered that since the weather had been decent today, maybe it won't be so bad in the tents tonight. Cheered by this thought we shouldered our packs to leave this beautiful corner of the County of Durham and head off into Cumbria. As we walked along the track to the last working farm in this lonely place the young couple jogged by and somehow we managed to prevent ourselves from joining in, or commenting, in any way, whatsoever.

Different strokes.

We reached Birkdale farm, which seemed incredibly remote. As we continued the moorland returned and the path alternated between bog and the occasional flagstones when the bog was more pronounced. We had left the Tees. That river roared down Cauldron Snout having been set free from the reservoir, which in turn is fed by the main gathering grounds below Cross Fell. Beside us is Maize Beck and today it was a gentle, friendly river.

A lone walker was striding towards us, who as he came closer we

**Looking back to Falcon Clints before saying goodbye to the Tees**

recognised as one of the group that we spoke to in the bar of the Teesdale Hotel last evening. He had a face like thunder and he did not acknowledge us. In the distance were two more men. One seemed to be swimming in the water of the beck, while the other was towelling down. Once we were within hailing distance we recognised the rest of the party from the bar. The man was still swimming and he told us that they had been up to High Cup, like we'd suggested and now on their return, he spotted this swimming opportunity and could not let it go by. He claimed that it was not as cold as it looked. Meanwhile his associate worked his towel in eloquent silence while trying to look enthusiastic.

Different strokes, indeed.

Ahead of us stood a large wooden bridge that crossed Maize Beck and led onto firmer ground on a higher path, south of the beck. We knew where we were, we knew what was coming but that was not the case forty years ago.

A while back there was a television programme about the Pennine

**Maize Beck**

**We knew where we were ...**

Way presented by Paul Rose. As on so many occasions when television tries 'to do' walking, it missed the mark by a long way. Except that when he came to High Cup the camera person had brought a drone which was flown slowly up the marshland of High Cup Plain allowing the view to appear as dramatically as it did for us all those years ago. The programme is worth seeing for that moment alone.

Somehow this time, the approach was different as this new route did not have the same reveal. Being slightly higher, we could see where a

**... we knew what was coming**

stream had cut a notch at the rim that gave a view of there being something beyond. Steadily the path led us to the edge before finally revealing the U-shaped valley. It still stopped us in our tracks.

High Cup is for walkers; there is no other route to it. It is the ultimate reward for walking up the valley from Middleton-in-Teesdale. On a good day the view is worth walking all the way from Edale to enjoy. Time has not diminished its perfection.

With a little imagination I could almost feel the ghost of the glacier

**Scrambling over the moraine**

scraping out the valley and being resisted by the tall hard basalt that buttresses the sides.

Below us we watched as a family scrambled across the moraine. Apparently there is a path that leads up beside the beck to where we are standing and it looked a gruelling task.

We lingered at this spot for over half an hour, not wanting this long awaited moment to end. But the practicalities of having a bed for the night and something to eat coaxed us to move on.

The path to Dufton first has to rise to meet the top of the basalt shelf. For some reason I missed the start of this and found myself embroiled with the escarpment below. Fortunately Chris corrected my course before anything too dangerous occurred. Safely on the path we made good time down to Dufton and the campsite. It was now about five thirty and we were the last of the walkers to find a pitch. Robin had already set up 'Big Agnes' and he poked his head out to let us

**High Cup Nick**

know that he'd been here for hours. He was not terribly impressed with today's walk, preferring to fixate on the heights of tomorrow.

There was another camper we'd not seen before who was sitting sullenly beside a highly technical 'coffin' tent. He confirmed his professional walker's credentials by tending a stove on which a pan full of grey pulses bubbled ominously. The kind of thing that people on expeditions a long way from fresh food might be forced to eat.

We set out our tents in the wet long grass as the shadows of the surrounding high trees stretched rapidly towards us. Chris headed to the shower. While he was in there I spotted a sign recommending that campers should book dinner in the pub but when I rang they either had a lot of bookings or a very tiny kitchen and therefore couldn't fit us in until eight o'clock. On Chris's return I made haste to the shower, which with the toilets was about a hundred yard dash from the camping area. Chris had discovered that there was hot water, thank goodness. However, the water was on a push tap that timed-out after a frugal fifteen seconds and the only way to enjoy a longer shower was to awkwardly lean backwards on the tap while showering.

There was only one cubicle so I showered using this technique. This was fine to start with, as I contorted my body forward to catch the stream of hot water. This inevitably lessened the pressure on the tap so the moment it started petering out my body temperature dropped. I leaned back to fully depress the tap and receive another quarter of a minute of warmth. After an awkward and uncomfortable shower I towelled down and changed into my evening wear before skedaddling back to the tent.

The campsite lacked facilities such as a drying room and my towel

**The route down from High Cup to Dufton in 1979**

was sopping wet. I laid it out on a wooden fence, although I didn't hold out any hope of any drying occurring as the sun had sunk behind the woods. Although the trees offered some protection for this end of the campsite from the constant wind, the cloudless sky promised a chilly night.

Dufton had only one contribution to the night time economy and though it was a bit early for us to eat, we headed to the pub. Standing at the bar we let them know we'd booked and they were adamant about the booking time. Never mind, we continued the pint and pork scratchings diet and sat down at the table reserved for us.

Simon was sitting eating his dinner nearby and we offered him a place on our table and he was happy to join us. For a change, he failed to ask if we'd been cheating again. Maybe because for any journey between Middleton-in-Teesdale and Dufton the path is the most direct route. Even though, perversely, we were now further away from our terminus at the end of the day than when we started (as every Pennine Way walker will tell you, sorry to do it again). Sitting in the warm embrace of the pub we discussed the glories of the day and I found that I had a certain grudging admiration for lone walkers as they have to find an answer for every eventuality. For the lone walker the Pennine Way is relentless and unforgiving and will expose the weaknesses in all who attempt it, whereas Chris and I can rely on each other for support.

Simon mentioned that he had some misgivings regarding his accommodation. He claimed that it was a bit of let down in standards especially after his experience of what he described as a 'five star b&b' that he'd stayed in the night before. Quick as a flash Chris offered to swap places with him and surprisingly for a short moment Simon mentally weighed up the pros and cons before declining.

My thoughts turned to where Rob was tonight. When he proffered his schedule to us over a week ago at the beginning of the Way, this was the day that made us worry for him. He was starting at Langdon Beck and had booked his next evening's accommodation in Alston, twenty-eight miles further on. He would have had to rush past all of this beauty and then face the long trek over Cross Fell.

The young couple arrived and they sat nearby for the next hour or two. They were booked in to eat at the same time as us but the system failed as one of the waiters took their order early. It was not our problem and we really didn't care that they had jumped ahead in the queue for food but it was amusing to watch the confusion this caused for the house.

This couple were the youngest of the walkers that we had met on the Way so far and they were in their mid-thirties. The other members of our cohort were men of a certain age, namely their fifties and probably thought to be having a mid-life crisis by their friends and partners. We don't qualify for this group as Chris and I were 'the old men of the Way' (although we would not claim to be the oldest to ever walk it). However we all began to wonder where the walkers of tomorrow will come from. In fact, where were the walkers of today because far from the bustling long-distance route that we were anticipating, the Way

was practically empty.

It had been a very different evening from the last time we were here. Then it was full to bursting with locals, drinking hard and playing darts. In amongst the bustle and noise I transgressed some unwritten rule of local etiquette and was aggressively asked if I was tired o' livin'. This evening in comparison had been one of peace and tranquility.

Simon headed back to his b&b and his blog, the couple headed off to the warmth of their Hobbit Hole. We tried to fortify ourselves for the night ahead with a wee dram.

It should have been antifreeze.

**Upper Teesdale**

Mapping:
https://www.wikiloc.com/hiking-trails/pw-11-dufton-to-alston-41056295

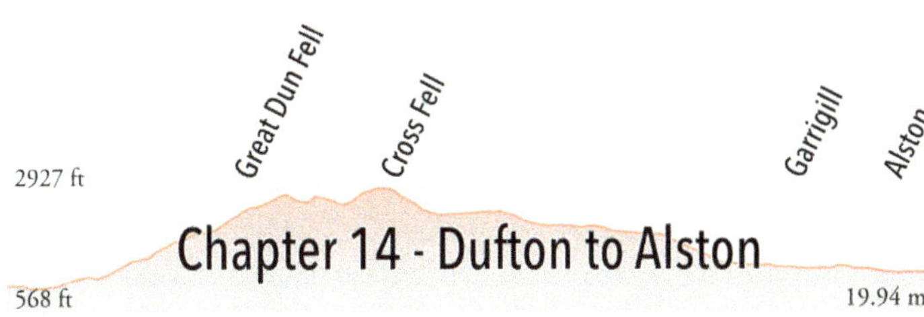


# Chapter 14 - Dufton to Alston

Total ascent: 21845 ft | Total distance: 179.02 miles

September 8th

**Chris:** Yesterday and today are two of the big days of the Pennine Way. The fresh memory of the most recent walk from Middleton to Dufton matched closely my recall of the 1979 version which is unusually for me, pretty clear, probably because it is a truly spectacular day. High Force and High Cup, just a few miles apart, are two of the best bits of scenery you'll find anywhere in England.

Today's walk, while not so attractive visually, is outstanding insofar as it takes us over Cross Fell, the highest terrain of the whole Pennine Way and indeed some of the highest land in England. Outstanding too because many consider Dufton to Alston the most demanding section of the whole two hundred and seventy miles. The ascent to Cross Fell via the taster climbs of Knock, Great Dun and Little Dun Fells is certainly a slog, and the largely downhill trudge to Garrigill and Alston beyond seems interminable, but I still feel that Day 1 and the final day (or days) crossing the Cheviots offer a greater challenge.

Whatever your opinion, the best way to prepare is not to spend an appallingly sleepless, very cold night in a tent.

We both rose early and emerged to find that the thick carpet of lush green grass of the campsite which would normally be welcomed as a comfort aid to someone sleeping on the floor, was in fact a reservoir containing millions of gallons of water which was impossible to avoid when crawling out of the tent. I for one had been freezing all night, despite wearing virtually every piece of clothing I had with me, and as

**Opposite: Great Dun Fell from the path leaving Dufton**

a result had barely slept a wink. Duncan seemed particularly unhappy with the experience and announced that he was definitely not camping any more. I had no arguments to offer.

While we whined, our neighbour Robin, with whom we were now chatting freely despite his previous reticence, packed up and was away on his characteristically early start. He had baffled us the night before by dismissing that day as nothing very special while getting excited about the day ahead – it was all about the height for him apparently. There's nowt so queer as folk as they may say in these parts (although we're probably on t' wrong side o' 'ills for that sort of talk).

The only café in the village doesn't open until ten, so the reader will no doubt be expecting to hear that our early dismay was compounded by the run of cooked breakfasts coming to an end. That would be to underestimate the resourcefulness of the authors however. Before we left Essex I had called a b&b in the village. Would they be prepared to provide us with just the second b? 'It's not something we normally do', the friendly lady had explained, but nevertheless she said we'd be welcome. So, packed and now feeling warmer, we strolled in the morning sun to our eight a.m. rendezvous with fry up number ten.

Tucking into his own plateful at the next table we found Simon, who it turned out, had availed himself of both b's at this very establishment. We were cheered to find that he too had had a bad night though for different reasons to us: it seems that only his tiredness and the lack of alternative had allowed him to put up with a perceived absence of cleanliness in his room. While he scratched, we enjoyed our breakfast and made the most of the warm bathroom facilities for a good – er – wash.

It was early for us then when we set out on the first of nearly twenty miles to be conquered, heading out of the village on a gently upward trajectory with the compact Dufton Pike to our right. Re-reading my original Wainwright (fifty-ninth impression), it is interesting to note that back then the steep slope of the Pike had been earmarked as a location for the development of a huge outdoor sports centre incorporating ski slopes, a hotel and restaurants. It is obvious from the general lack of facilities in Dufton today that such a development had never happened: it would surely have had a massive effect on the commercial life of the village. As it is, this lovely countryside remains unchanged, one thing at least that would have Wainwright *not* spinning in his grave.

We both remembered that the climb to Knock Fell was a serious one and at Swindale Beck we took another 'cheating' decision, allowing us to avoid Knock Fell altogether. Branching off across a slightly gentler gradient we joined and then followed a small road, allegedly the highest in England, which snaked its way to the summit of Great Dun Fell. Well maintained but private, the road provides access to a radar station that sits atop the Fell, and whose spherical white 'radome' is visible for miles.

**It's a radome, apparently**

The steep ascent was slow and arduous but we were entertained by the thought that by dint of this shortcut we might now be ahead of Simon. This alternative route is actually one that Wainwright recommends in bad weather, but for once the weather was behaving; we were not being rained on though the temperature remained low and the wind high. Massive cloud formations built all around us, continuously changing and combining with a beautiful azure sky to provide us with a series of fabulous skyscapes as we neared the first of the day's summits.

There's a sense on this day's walk that the climb to Great Dun Fell is just the first bit, the early part of the walk, but it was nearly midday by the time we finally arrived at the radar

**Fabulous, ever-changing skyscapes**

station. We stopped for a short breather, nodding helloes to cyclists and motorcyclists for whom the fell's summit has become a destination, thanks to the excellent road, but soon pushed on down the northern slope. From there the next challenges were clearly visible: Little Dun Fell first, and then looming beyond, intermittently shrouded in cloud, was the big one, Cross Fell.

The dips between the fells tend to bogginess so we were pleased to see more slabs taking us across these areas; smaller than the huge ones that we saw back on that first day but still making good progress easy. Within an hour we were up and over Little Dun Fell and had summited Cross Fell. The cloud had lifted making visibility in all directions good and the walk along the top of the fell was exhilarating.

**Looking back to Great Dun Fell from the plateau on Cross Fell**

The three sixty panorama of northern England's highest regions is special, and progress was fairly slow for a while as we took in the full extent of this tremendous place. Numerous cairns provided us with hints to the way ahead across the desolate, otherwise empty plateau. Although we'd loved the previous day, it was easy to see why Robin would be excited by the prospect of reaching this point.

Cross Fell is known for a special wind, the Helm, England's only, as its always described, 'named wind'. A strong north easterly, the Helm blows when a complicated set of meteorological conditions combine, and can be destructive when it hits the settlements on the western side of the fell. Such conditions most frequently occur earlier in the year though, and the wind we were experiencing, which had brought us so much rain over the preceding days was a westerly and decidedly not the Helm. It did however continue to buffet us as we arrived at the shelter that marks the highest point on the fell, and a natural place to take a break. While we did so a young family with a baby arrived, taking advantage of the shelter to change the infant's nappy. Start 'em young I say.

A short break and on to the afternoon's long descent to Garrigill. This bit of the walk has stayed with me from '79 in the form of images of dry, dusty paths, relentless hot sunshine and being thirsty as we came down from the three thousand feet of Cross Fell to eleven hundred at Garrigill. A significant descent, but completed over a distance of about six miles so it's anything but a steep gradient overall.

It starts with a steepish bit like the downward slopes of the earlier fells, and continues into a broad area of boggy terrain. We were by now used to the twenty-first century Pennine Way paths being distinct and easy to follow, but here we failed to find an obvious route across the bog. Perhaps we came off the fell at the wrong point, but according to the OS on my phone we were bang on the path, though we could see nothing around us to corroborate this. There were no other people to be seen either which was perplexing as there had been a few walkers we'd noted ahead of us during the morning, and as we tried to progress we appeared to be getting into more and more difficult and wetter terrain. Duncan seemed to be getting into more trouble than me, struggling to find a route back towards where I was and becoming quite concerned. It was all a bit baffling and looking now at the maps and aerial photographs of this small area it continues to be so: we still don't understand how a short walk down from the fell to the well-formed and visible track heading to Garrigill became so difficult. We even wondered if somehow the route had been changed, but eventually we hit the track. Soon after, the appearance of Greg's Hut, an old mining building now restored to provide shelter for walkers, reassured us that we were where we should be and we were comfortable again.

**In '79 there was a colourful alternative to Greg's Hut**

At this point the Pennine Wayer might feel that they've broken the back of this day's walk but actually Greg's Hut pops up at just nine miles, Alston being still more than that distance away. However, the wide, good quality path enabling us to walk two abreast, the gentle descent and decent weather were conducive to conversation and so we were able to have a good old chat as we strode along at a very respectable pace.

After a walk with Duncan or the boys, I'm often asked by Mag 'what did you talk about?' There will usually have been a wide range of topics – we all always like to hear how the others' offspring are doing, and being blokes there'll be some discussion of football/rugby/cricket at some point. There might be a little bit of politics occasionally, and as everyone has their own little area of knowledge and experience all sorts of other subjects readily pop up and usually, everyone will have an opinion to share.

I think I am known for talking about, or very possibly droning on endlessly about, work. For the last twenty years of my full time working life, business partner Mike and I ran our own business, employing at the peak over forty people involved one way or another in the provision of photographic services to the medical sector. I never succumbed to workaholism but for all of those twenty years I put in much more than the forty hour week and almost inevitably I suppose, the issues and challenges I experienced on a daily basis filled my consciousness and hence my conversation.

Contracting to the NHS as we did became more and more challenging over the years and two years before this Pennine Way trip Mike and I decided to call it a day. Mike retired completely, but a couple of months after we downed tools, I was asked back by one of the hospitals we had previously contracted to, to work one day a week with dermatology and ENT patients. This gig had continued to the present day – I was at the hospital the day before we left for Edale – but now the dermatologists were looking to expand their activity into skin cancer photo-triage, and were keen to have my involvement.

I was keen to be involved too: using photography to improve diagnostic procedures for an increasingly prevalent form of cancer seemed like an obvious and very worthwhile use of my skills. Consequently, my work once again became a topic of conversation as throughout the afternoon my phone bonged with the opening salvo of a number of communications from the hospital that I would receive during this second half of the walk. It seemed that they wanted to get the new service off the ground urgently and I found myself agreeing to a three day week starting immediately after the Friday we planned to hit Kirk Yetholm. I could tell that Duncan thought I must be slightly mad agreeing to this and I must say I agreed to it with a hint of nervousness: not only did it mean we had to finish on time but also not carrying any injury that might prevent me working.

Another regular topic of conversation for the two of us of course, is the past and what we remember of the first time on this walk. Broadly our memories coincide, but it is surprising and sometimes baffling how they differ. For years I remembered clearly that in 1979 we had opted out of scaling Pen-y-Ghent, a 'fact' that when I mentioned it to Duncan more recently was hotly disputed. Privately I retained the view that I was right until just a few weeks before this trip when I found a photograph I had taken, captioned, in my own hand, 'On Pen-y-Ghent 24/8/79'. On it, not skirting around the lower slopes to avoid a big climb.

There are many things that we both remember clearly however, one being the little shop in Garrigill that sold ice cream, wonderfully welcome on that hot, dry day. Hoping we'd be able to repeat that pleasure, we continued along what was by now a very well maintained track, probably we thought, suggestive of some commercial activity. We understood that some of the mineral deposits, once mined extensively in these parts, especially in the mid to late nineteenth century were now being exploited again and guessed that that had led to the upgrading of the track.

The industrial history of this part of the Pennines is well known and documented, it having been a rich source of lead ore particularly. Although now much naturalised, the landscape here is marked with the scars of old mine workings and spoil heaps. As we walked along the stony path we regularly spotted small fragments of fluorspar, an attractive blue mineral which was mined here and used in processing the lead. If there was any such work going on now however, there were no people to provide evidence of it and the long descent to Garrigill, which every now and then threw up a bit of ascent, was a lonely one.

Our glorious arrival at Garrigill was not celebrated with ice cream.

Unfortunately the shop was closed – not surprising really as it was by now late Sunday afternoon - so we walked on pausing only for a brief exchange with a cycling toddler whose mum was chatting nearby. The village was very quiet but in its day it would have been much busier, apparently with a population five times what it is today, having been home to the many lead miners. Today, like so many rural communities the village cannot sustain shops, pubs and the like, so although it may perhaps seem a more likely place to end the day's walk, continuing to Alston makes more sense.

For anyone who really does want to stay in the village there is accommodation in the form of camping and a bunkhouse at the village hall, but you'd have to be carrying your food for evening and breakfast. For us though, once again a quick google and a telephone call secured a twin room, this time at the Angel Inn in Alston.

The final four miles to Alston taken alone is an undemanding valley walk, but coming after the fifteen already walked it is one that anyone would wish to be over sooner than it seems to be.

**The last few miles is undemanding: the pleasant South Tyne**

Firstly the path heads northwest along the pleasant west bank of the South Tyne before crossing the river and continuing on at a steady height above the valley bottom. There was little ascent or descent, for which we were grateful. After a couple of miles through lush, pleasant farmland with small fields and a gate or stile to negotiate seemingly about every hundred yards, the path became a well formed track and in turn a small road that suddenly delivered us through the trees to Alston.

It was nearing six o'clock by the time we were sitting in the Angel having a refreshing end of walk pint and a bit beyond seven when, settled in and showered, we went for a stroll around the town centre. Both of us remembered Alston as a busy little place but this evening, apart from an unpleasant shouting match going on outside the other pub, there were few signs of life. Not, it should be said, that we were looking for nightlife: we were I think as tired as we had been so far and settling back into the Angel for a couple of drinks, something to eat and bed was about all we were good for.

**Alston, on a hazy day in 1979**

Mapping:
https://www.wikiloc.com/hiking-trails/pw-12-alston-to-greenhead-41679065

Epiacum
Langley Viaduct
Wain Rigg
Greenhead

1128 ft

# Chapter 15 - Alston to Greenhead

438 ft
16.52 mi

Total ascent: 23138 ft
Total distance: 195.54 miles

September 9th

**Chris:** Yesterday, while heading towards the day's big challenge of Cross Fell, with thoughts of the days ahead and particularly Hadrian's Wall, an image of the lone tree growing in Sycamore Gap, near Housesteads fort on the amazing Roman construction, came into my mind. It's an image that would probably be called 'iconic' these days: certainly it's a photograph that's been taken by countless visitors to the Wall. And it is obvious why – a single tree in a dip between two almost symmetrically rising small hills placed by nature against a backdrop of empty sky, providing a scene of photogenic geometry.

The image that entered my mind was a specific version which, printed large, had been screwed to a waiting area wall in the hospital where I'd worked for those twenty years prior to the closure of our business. The picture was one of a dozen or so rural views that we had enlarged for display in order to brighten up the otherwise fairly dismal basement area we worked in. They were all taken by one of our team, James, who as well as being employed by my company as a medical photographer is also a talented landscape photographer. His Sycamore Gap captured a sunny, golden, autumnal day, the lack of people in the shot suggestive of a remote, lonely place, even though there were probably hundreds of visitors within yards.

This James had come to us in his early twenties, soon after

**Sycamore Gap**
**Courtesy of James (www.jamesnormanphoto.com)**

completing a photography degree. He was quite a shy young man, but he soon proved himself, becoming a first rate medical photographer and a loyal, hard working employee as well as just being a lovely guy to have around. Having gathered a good knowledge of all the work we medical photographers do, he left us after a few years seeking further opportunities for development and seniority, and eventually took a job back in the north of England, returning to live at his family home. If at this point I mention that the family home is in Haltwhistle, no more than three miles from Greenhead, the end of today's walk, the imaginative reader might realise where this historical preamble is leading.

I last caught up with James in the summer of 2017. To mark the end not only of the business but also of our forty years as medical photographers, Mike and I hosted a party (we were always good at parties) to which all of our current and previous employees were invited. James trekked down from Northumberland to be there and make his contribution to what was a great night. Now, a couple of years later I texted him from Little Dun Fell to let him know that we were heading his way, thinking that it might be nice to have a pint with him as we would be holing up somewhere in the vicinity of Greenhead. It turned into much more than just a pint.

**Duncan:** Chris was sure I would remember James because I had worked with him once and since I struggle to put a name to a face at the best of times, I asked Chris to remind me of the circumstances.

Chris had asked to me to film an eye operation and James was tasked to assist me. The main problem with attempting to film any operative procedure is that the camera generally needs to be where the surgeon's head is and (since they have yet to design surgeons with see through heads) for a successful outcome the surgeon needs to be ready to make compromises. The main skill, having sorted out the camera position is tactfully reminding the surgeon to conduct the operation without obscuring the view for the length of the procedure.

I barely remembered James because although physically present he was unobtrusive, only speaking when spoken to and seemingly lacking inquisitiveness. However I could tell by the glowing way that Chris was talking about him today that James must have blossomed into a very capable member of the team.

**Chris:** First though, the journey to Greenhead. The breakfast part of the Angel's b&b offering was provided in a small back room which seemed more like – and probably was – the landlady's private dining room, at a single table with all of the other residents.

From an intrepid looking chap who was on the Way heading north to south, we heard, not for the first time that for us it was 'all bog from here' to Kirk Yetholm. We knew that this wasn't totally true, but it did remind us that the general wetness northern England had experienced this year must have had an effect on the terrain and we did expect to encounter plenty of messy ground. Having said that, this chap, anticipating a lack of drinkable water was carrying four litres of the stuff which to us seemed more than mildly excessive, so perhaps his judgement generally was suspect. Note to any walkers planning their Pennine Way adventure – four litres of water weighs four kilograms, the carrying of which is not necessary or even slightly sensible. (Get yourself a water bottle with a filter so if you have to you can collect some river water!)

Replete once again with an excellent breakfast, we ventured out into the dull Alston morning which was grey but not yet raining. It was chilly though, not at all what might be expected of an early September day and we were both sporting more layers than just the walking shirt. We called in at the busiest place in town, the petrol station and bought some provisions – lunch and ibuprofen! – and were soon off along the A686 to a road bridge that took us over the South Tyne. Turning immediately to the north we were back on the path, alongside the river in whose attractive valley much of the morning's walk would be.

The walking was easy, staying more or less at the same height above the valley bottom for some time before the path gradually made its

**Views around Epiacum Roman Fort**

way down to the level of the river. By about eleven o'clock we'd reached the remains of Epiacum, a Roman fort shown on the OS as Whitley Castle. We stood for a moment to take it in – that's all it took frankly, not a lot to see, even for someone continually impressed by what the Romans did for us – and at the same time decided that the

wet stuff falling on us was set in for a while, so once again the rain gear went on.

As we walked we chatted about James and how the text conversation I'd had with him had turned in to an invitation not just for a pint but to stay with him in Haltwhistle. I'd accepted gladly on behalf of the pair of us, due mainly to the fact that we had until then anticipated spending the night at the Greenhead bunkhouse. Now as bunkhouses go, I'm sure that Greenhead's is one of the best, but its main characteristic is that it's a bunkhouse. We'd experienced the Horton one and been very, very grateful that we were the only residents, but a bunkhouse shared with who knows how many people held a level of attraction on a par with that of camping.

The scheduling of this day had been tricky: Greenhead is about sixteen miles from Alston and the first sensible stopping place, but we would ideally have gone a little further in order to reduce the inevitably long following day to Bellingham. However, all of the options at nearer to twenty miles that I looked at during planning were already fully booked, presumably a function of being close to Hadrian's Wall, a popular destination. The Sill YHA at Twice Brewed, nearly eight miles further on from Greenhead seemed a bit too far for one day. Forty years ago we'd simply wild camped in a field of cows somewhere near the Wall – what lightweights we've become. According to the Accommodation Record in my original Wainwright, we identified that spot as Burnhead, some four miles beyond Greenhead.

That day forty years ago seemed a very long one; the sun was fairly low in the sky by the time we'd camped, cooked and eaten. When we settled down into our sleeping bags with Radio 1 for late night company, DJ John Peel was playing a collection of his favourite songs to mark his birthday. The detail of this I hadn't recalled but of course it can now be read about online. It was actually his fortieth birthday, and in celebration he was playing his personal top forty. He apparently ended the show by playing 'the best one of the lot', the Kop Choir of his beloved Liverpool Football Club singing 'You'll never walk alone'. I'm sure if we were still awake at that point we would both have roundly abused Mr Peel for this choice.

The invitation from James had developed even further over a few more rounds of messaging and some clarification had been obtained: he was actually inviting us to stay with his parents. While I'd happily accepted his offer initially, I was less certain about accepting an invitation to stay with a third party who I didn't know, and uncomfortable about imposing on these unsuspecting people. James insisted we shouldn't worry, telling us his mum and dad loved walking, and predicting that they would 'chew our ears off' to find out everything there was to know about the Pennine Way and our experience of it. It was also true that whereas James is not much older than my firstborn, his parents are our contemporaries, born just like

**One of many viaducts along this part of the Way**

Duncan and I in the fifties, so we should have some common ground. And at the back of my mind I had memories from when James worked with us that other colleagues who'd visited his parents' home had reported that they were indeed lovely people and extended only the best hospitality, so we forced ourselves to accept what the coming night would bring.

### On the River Tyne Trail

Numerous trails weave their way through South Tynedale, sharing their routes intermittently with the Pennine Way: there's the River Tyne Trail, the South Tyne Trail, A Pennine Journey and even Isaac's Tea Trail. On the OS map of the area, it can be confusing working out which path is which, and for a while after Epiacum we followed the South Tyne Trail as far as Slaggyford. In retrospect I realise that my mapping followed the wrong route and we were denied the pleasure of walking alongside the river for a couple of miles: Wainwright describes the South Tyne as a 'beautiful river'.

Looking at the map now I think that following the River Tyne Trail all the way from Alston to Lambley is probably the most attractive of the alternatives through this valley, if not necessarily one for the Pennine Way purist. Nevertheless, the walk was pleasant if unspectacular, and the odd bit of sunshine occasionally lightened the grey, intermittently rainy morning.

It wasn't a mistake however when at Burnstones we took the decision over a brief lunch not to follow the planned route up the slight climb onto Lambley Common. Anticipating boggy terrain there, we stuck instead with the River Tyne Trail as far as Lambley, where the decision was rewarded by the sight of the tremendous viaduct across the river. The view was really worth the detour and we wondered why on earth the published Pennine Way route doesn't go this way. We'd certainly recommend it, although we could already hear Simon's voice haranguing us again.

Leaving Lambley we'd covered nearly two thirds of the day's walk but we anticipated that the remaining third would be far less enjoyable. It was just a short walk to get back on to the Pennine Way proper and soon we were heading north on a rolling but gradually climbing gradient towards Hartleyburn Common and on to Blenkinsopp Common beyond.

In the early afternoon gloom the view from the A689 Carlisle road was very uninviting. As we headed across the introductory Riggs of Holly and Dodd's we got a taste of what the soon to come Wain Rigg would offer. There used to be a London Underground announcer who would describe the profusion of 'Actons' on the Central Line by informing the travelling public that there were 'a lot of Actons'. If he were to find himself here, I'm sure he'd say 'a lot of riggs': the OS shows at least a dozen bits of land in this area with rigg in the name.

Often such words in names suggest a particular type of terrain but I'm given to understand that rigg is just an old word for ridge, which doesn't really describe what was ahead of us. If it meant areas of very wet, boggy ground rising gently out of absolutely sodden boggy ground it would be more accurate. Even at the time of writing, months later, the two short words Wain Rigg conjure up images of a slog across

**Holly, Dodd or Wain it's definitely a Rigg**

desolate, pathless, featureless, sludgy moorland on a heavily overcast, rainy, cold afternoon. As Wainwright puts it, if the rest of the Pennine Way were the same, this would be the place 'to pack it in and go home'.

There is no challenging gradient, but despite that progress was slow and tedious, for much of the time a matter of stepping from tussock to tussock trying to avoid the soggiest ground. It's not enjoyable walking, especially if like Duncan, you are finding that your new boots, bought on the recommendation of the man in the shop who said that they'd definitely do the Pennine Way, are giving poor grip and you are slipping, skidding and doing the splits on a regular basis.

Routefinding on this whole section from Lambley onwards is difficult too, depending on a few scattered posts which roughly indicate the way. At least with our twenty-first century tech we knew exactly where we were and so able to keep going in generally the right direction, close to, if not exactly on the path.

Somewhere on Wain Rigg, Duncan's mobile phone had the electronic equivalent of a seizure and suddenly at loud volume began to emit Radio 5 Live. It was as if the phone was itself so outraged by Johnson's 'prorogation' of Parliament that it had to make sure we knew about it as soon as possible. Further examination of the device revealed that the navigation app had gone crazy too and ultimately only a complete reset was going to get it going normally again. That meant that some of the route recordings Duncan had made would be lost: annoying, but not the end of the world and certainly not a level of tech failure that in any way impacted our progress.

Thankfully, the vileness of Wain Rigg lasted only a few miles, so after an admittedly fairly miserable couple of hours we attained the highest point around and drier terrain. Then it was just a couple of miles of unspectacular descent to the A69 Carlisle to Newcastle road, the crossing of which meant we were only minutes away from Greenhead.

We'd been keeping James informed of our progress throughout the day. He was aiming to pick us up in Greenhead as he drove home from Carlisle at the end of his working day, but we found ourselves in the centre of the village rather early in terms of the planned rendezvous. We therefore had no alternative but to position ourselves at the bar of the conveniently available Greenhead Hotel and sink a couple while we awaited his arrival.

The pub was quiet when we first arrived but soon familiar faces seemed to be joining us from all directions. As we hadn't seen Simon or Robin in Alston, I was surprised to see them here and enjoyed the opportunity to catch up. I'd imagined that as we progressed further north we'd gradually fall out of sync, but here they were. We also made the acquaintance of another couple, a male/female partnership who were the first walkers we've met who were using one of the companies who move your stuff for you - or as Simon put it in an aside to us - 'cheating'.

The camaraderie that develops between those progressing along the Way at roughly the same speed is one of the highlights of the walk; not only does it provide company for the evenings, chatting over a couple of beers (let's face it there's not much else to do most nights), reliving the highs and lows of the day but it can also lay the foundations of long lasting associations and friendships. Simon will no doubt recall inviting us to stay in his holiday let in Derbyshire any time, at highly preferential mates' rates.

In due course, James arrived and we loaded our gear into his car and getting into the back of it, apologised to his wife, Georgina, for what we imagined was our unpleasant smell. She only had a few minutes to endure it because we were soon on the doorstep of his parents' house. Half an hour later we were still on the doorstep - well, perhaps we'd progressed to just inside - as Helen and Stewart, James' parents, made good on his promise and held us in place with a barrage of questions about our experiences on the Way to date, when we planned to finish, where we'd stayed, how we'd prepared and well, not everything else, because there was the rest of the evening for that.

They eventually introduced us to their lovely home and our rooms, my one containing the biggest bed I'd ever slept in. While we showered, Helen busied herself not only cooking us an immense and delicious meal but also washing all our sodden and smelly clothing, way beyond the call of duty. Our American friend Robin had walked the Appalachian Trail, one of the great US walks and he'd spoken of 'the kindness of strangers' when recalling his abiding memory of it: the phrase he'd used sprang to mind now.

Over the exceptional meal, for which James and Georgina joined us, conversation about walking and the Pennine Way never abated save for the occasional mention of the professional history James and I shared, and indeed, continued when we eventually relocated, replete, to the lounge. Here, as if we hadn't been spoiled enough already, the whisky decanter was introduced to the proceedings and another hour or so of talking took place in front of a roaring wood fire.

With the warmth, comfort and alcohol the two of us had the most relaxing evening we could possibly have imagined. Better than that bunkhouse I'm sure. Eventually our beds called and with the promise of Stewart's speciality porridge breakfast in mind, I for one slept like a log.

Mapping:
https://www.wikiloc.com/hiking-trails/pw-13-greenhead-to-bellingham-40388560

Cattle graze beside the Wall

# Chapter 16 - Greenhead to Bellingham

Total ascent: 25507 ft Total distance: 217.05 miles

September 10th

**Duncan:** What a rare day, to wake up feeling guilty but oh, oh so pleased. No dream could be bettered by the reality of the kindness of strangers that we had received over the previous evening but now sadly it will end. Downstairs, Stewart was in the kitchen tending to a pot of porridge while Helen was in the front room checking on our clothes that were drying on an airer by the embers of last night's fire. I felt like a teenager, having my cares and worries tended by responsible adults, instead of the old man that I so obviously am.

We gladly accepted the porridge and sat down to be presented with a cup of freshly brewed coffee, all this is rounded off with lashings of toast. It's like an Enid Blyton story except occasionally something happens. They asked where we were aiming to stay tonight. Bellingham was our target, the only obvious stopping point with a pub and accommodation (note the order of importance). Of course we didn't have anything booked but since we are now officially *not* using the tents our previous plan of heading for the campsite was out of the question. I took out my phone and began to look at the options which, because all the b&b places were already fully booked, were: 1) the bunkhouse, which after our experience in Horton-in-Ribblesdale was merely of academic interest as we now considered them an even less attractive proposition than the tents, or 2) a farmhouse some two miles to the east and nowhere near the Pennine Way. Unless we were ready to walk even further today it looked as though the retirement of the tents may have been premature.

Our hosts meanwhile are delighted because they tell us they would love nothing more than to pick us up from Bellingham and bring us back to their house to do this all over again. We can't accept this, everything we've experienced since we arrived in Haltwhistle had been above and beyond. They argued that they have enjoyed our company, even been inspired by us to walk, to explore and experience the local countryside and they really would like nothing more than for us to stay another day. I would like to say that this was a really hard decision, that we could not possibly accept this hospitality, that this was an imposition too far…

However, Helen and Stewart were such lovely hosts it was impossible to say no.

In truth, this was not a hard decision to make because not only did it solve one of the major conundrums of the way ahead, it would also mean that for one more day we could walk without a full pack. We cannot thank them enough for their hospitality and pop back upstairs to hastily unpack before they changed their minds.

At a quarter to ten, Stewart dropped us opposite the Greenhead Hotel, we took our packs and agreed to send him a message when we're about an hour away from Bellingham. We headed off, firstly through scrubby farmland until the trail turned north. Ahead of us were many walkers on an elevated path and when we reached the Wall the popularity of this route became very apparent. At some of the stiles there were queues and as we passed the car parks, large groups were milling about between the cars and coaches, marshalled by guides. Many languages could be heard and the cheery greeting that we gave to each passing walker and group was returned in a variety of accents and languages.

Hadrian's Wall follows a ridge of hard rock known as the Sill that rises and falls to the far horizon. Each individual peak and trough amounts to a minor hill or valley but over the miles a large amount of climbing is accomplished. This is a deceptively hard walk but on an excellent path.

After an hour we arrived at Burnhead where, as Chris mentioned,

*Chapter Sixteen*

# The Wall and the Sill

**Burnhead in 1979**

forty years earlier with dusk settling in and after walking over twenty-three miles, we gave up trying to reach the Twice Brewed youth hostel, still three or four miles distant and wild camped beside the Wall. The next morning we awoke to a dense fog which shrouded the view.

Today, the two thousand year old stone wall is no longer an obstacle to marauding Picts and was our constant companion. The line of stones scrambling over the undulating hills to the far horizon was a truly inspiring sight. Along the Way we passed several Roman

and 2019

milecastles, small structures where sentries would shelter and it seems that the Roman mile was very similar to a present day English one. The old imperial system of feet, yards and miles was built to a human scale over time and somehow, when walking, miles seem a more accurate description of distance and feet a better representation of height than kilometres and metres.

Freed from our heavy packs we made good time to the famous Sycamore Gap. After eight miles in the company of the glorious wall and just before the ruins of Housesteads, the Pennine

**Sycamore Gap**

Way heads northward. According to all the guidebooks, we should take the detour to see the best preserved Roman fort in Britain but that is a trip for another day as there are many more miles to cover before dinner.

Leaving the wall is a difficult moment because it is here that the Pennine Way loses its meaning. The last of the Pennine hills petered out when the Wall was reached and indeed since Alston, the path has taken an odd route which many people have questioned. Ahead are the vast forests of Northumberland, interspersed with flat featureless moorland and despite all the miles already completed it is right now that many wonder at the point of the Pennine Way.

Wainwright felt that Hadrian's Wall would make a more fitting ending to the Way and back in 1938 when he undertook the walk that he documented in his book 'A Pennine Journey', he trod this part of the Wall before returning south. There is a very good argument for continuing to Housesteads, then turning back south to Vindolanda to see the museum, before heading down to Bardon Mill to catch a train home. It would definitely make a fuller and more inspiring ending than mooching into a Scottish border town with minimal public transport options after a twenty seven mile hike.

Once more, I have digressed. The Pennine Way heads waywardly and inexorably north and despite our capacity for free thought we continued with it.

**Who doesn't love a pointless stile**

Immediately there was a marked deterioration in the path as we left the hard rock of the Sill and headed into the valley where sphagnum moss and bog sedges abound.

I looked at my lightweight boots; they've had the kitchen sink thrown at them over the last two weeks and as the bogginess of the land increased I could see a problem arising. In order to explain this I am going to have to get a bit technical because parts of my boots were coming apart that shouldn't. My boots look like you would expect. They had an 'outsole' which was the bit that touches the ground and a boot 'upper' which was the bit that wraps around the foot and ankle and in this case, a boot 'lower' which was a moulded rubber shell that connects to the sole and was welded to the side of the boot 'upper'. The problem was that the boot 'lower' was coming apart from the 'upper' and from my viewpoint as the sides flexed with each step I could see water sloshing around. I seemed to be walking with a personal aquarium. This was happening not just on one side of my

**Sitka spruce cones**

boot but the other as well and not merely on one boot but both of my boots. Despite this disheartening flaw my feet were not wet at the moment, but the forecast was not good.

There was nothing I could do to rectify this so we ploughed on, quickly approaching the first of the large forestry plantations. We were entering a desert of Sitka spruce. Some of the stands had been recently cleared, leaving row after row of bleached stumps that resembled a giant cornfield which had been ravaged by a monstrous combine harvester. In other places the stumps have new trees unhappily planted in amongst them. Then there were fields of young trees swaying in the wind, alive with the promise of youth and finally the large trees, cramped and tall, towering over everything else, awaiting the forester's chainsaw. It was strange and unsettling to see such stepped uniformity.

How very different it would have been thousands of years ago before the land was cleared, when we would have walked through a canopy of dense natural forest filled with birdsong. The American walker Robin told us that when he was walking the Appalachian Way it was often spoken of as 'the green tunnel' because the forests are endless. Today, the ancient forests of Britain are a rare sight and the fake forests of Kielder are in comparison, tragically, a wildlife desert, despite the greenwash of the Forest Park Authority.

At a fork in the path we came across the couple that we had met the night before in the bar of the Greenhead Hotel. They were eating their packed lunch in a sunny glade and we stopped to talk. Chris's phone rang and while he dealt with some work-related problem I chatted to them about the day so far. They didn't enjoy Hadrian's Wall, too much up and down, they felt. I countered with the 'walking on history' argument but they remained unconvinced.

I asked them which way the path goes and they obligingly pointed to our left. I rejoined Chris as he finished his call and we followed their prompt and headed off in what turned out to be the wrong direction. Under normal circumstances it would only have been a few yards before Wikiloc pointed out the error but after the wetness of yesterday on Wain Rigg, my phone was not working properly and the audible warning that we'd left the route didn't come.

It wasn't until several minutes later that I checked the route, only to find that the forest track we were following had veered away from the Pennine Way. Fortunately there was a path ahead that would lead us back, so we settled down to a lunch of biscuits and water in the sunshine, before tramping through a disused quarry that held a surprisingly pleasant forest glade of mixed woodland hidden in amongst the serried ranks of Sitka.

As we turned north to continue the Way, behind us we could see the couple that we'd met earlier and coming towards us were three walkers. They revealed themselves to be north-southers, that rare breed of hardy Pennine Way walkers.

'It's all bog from here on.' they laughed as they passed.

'You'll enjoy tomorrow then' I replied, thinking of Wain Rigg.

I have to wonder what is the attraction for walking the Way in reverse. Since journalist and campaigner Tom Stephenson first postulated the route of Pennine Way in 1935, the natural progression was assumed to lead towards certain features, Malham Cove for example. Coming from the opposite direction would mean approaching the lip, then admiring the view, descending the steps and walking away from the Cove. The view of the Cove is always over one's shoulder. This would be even worse on the Dufton to Middleton day. Starting with a walk up to High Cup that would lack the drama of the original route, then scrambling down Cauldron Snout and walking away from High and Low Force. That would be a terrible shame. Not to mention that the weather which generally prevails from the west is much more in the face of the north south walker. These walkers don't seem to care though.

In this forest, where the trees were packed tightly together, I would have expected the moisture to be sucked out of the ground. The reality could not have been more of a contrast as somehow the water skated

**Hurrying to the 'Pit Stop'**

off the pine leaves and was corralled under the trees, rendering the paths as sloppy as any bog. Consequently I was floundering like a hopeless drunk.

The staggered miles passed and so finally did the forest because the Pennine Way only touches a small corner of the vast Kielder Water and Forest Park and now we were back to more rural farmland and bog. We passed several badly made signs that told us that we were nearing the 'Pit Stop' and the thought of taking a rest and enjoying some sugared treats and maybe even a cold drink, kept us moving.

Back in '79 it was common to see a sign at a farm gate offering tea or coffee to passing walkers. We would stop for a hot drink, maybe some home made cake and what would often turn out to be a long conversation with the local farmer. The slow stranglehold of regulation has brought an end to this enterprise as it is now necessary to have food safety certificates for the simple task of making a cuppa. These days we occasionally came across 'Tuck shops', a box or cold store where kind people placed a few cold drinks and snacks for a suggested donation. At Horneystead Farm the whole operation was taken up a level. The signs led to the back of the buildings and into a room where there was a kettle, a motley selection of comestibles and some old armchairs that look like they'd been bequeathed from a house where a mad cat woman had died. There was also a toilet which is always a good thing to find. All these facilities were for the use of passing walkers. We perused the various offerings and decided to buy some sweets that we remembered liking as children before moving on.

In the next few moments we realised that either we had no sense of taste when we were kids, or the recipe had been significantly altered over the years. Whatever had happened and despite the fact that we really no longer found these sweetmeats palatable, there was a strong feeling that we should be grateful anyway for the kindness and enterprise of the farmer and so we ate them. Although it was more likely that our bodies were just desperate for the calories.

It was farmland from now on, apart from a slight diversion over a

**Shitlington sheep. A Leicester cross, I'm told and I would be too if I was known as a Shitlington**

hard rocky outcrop with the unfortunate name of Shitlington Crags. From these heights we looked across to the valley beyond. We were about an hour from finishing so we texted Stewart to let him know that we were nearly there.

Walking into the valley, the little town of Bellingham slowly revealed itself as we headed towards the main road. We happily passed the campsite where we would have stayed and just as we reached the bridge that crosses the North Tyne, Stewart appeared in his red car. We should really walk the final few yards to the town centre except it would be rude to not accept the lift.

For the past few hours I'd been worrying about my boots. Although they'd kept the water at bay so far, I didn't believe it would be long before they failed. I asked Stewart if he had some adhesive back at his home that I could use to patch them up. Araldite would have a fighting chance of sticking the sides back together. (This probably isn't the best advertisement for it but when one of the masters at my school wanted to put up a notice board in his form room, he famously stated with tremendous confidence that 'Araldite will do it boys, they stuck airplanes together with it during the war.' Naturally, to much hilarity, it fell off the wall a couple of days later. Young hands may have intervened to ease it away.) However my father always used it for tough jobs and so have I. Stewart was not sure if he had Araldite, or indeed adhesive of any type that could be used in this situation, especially as most people's standby, Superglue is generally not so much of a glue in the presence of water. He phoned James and together they hatched a plan to help me out.

Arriving home we were met by James who was holding the largest tin of contact adhesive I had ever seen. Two and a half litres of the stuff. Probably enough to get every glue sniffer in England as high as a kite. I was pondering just how much of the national debt he had invested in this tin when he stated that he found it in Georgina's grandfather's shed.

I looked at the instructions and the most glaring point was that the surfaces to be bonded must be clean and dry. After thirteen days of walking these were probably the last two adjectives that could be used to describe my boots. Helen found some cotton buds and paper towels and I began the task of clearing out the boggy detritus, while Stewart said he would get a fire going so I could dry them out. I seemingly sluiced away a swimming pool's worth of water and extracted a few Sitka spruce before settling the boots on some newspaper beside the fire.

After a shower and a change of clothes we returned to the kitchen where Stewart was cracking open some beers, safe in the knowledge that we wouldn't refuse them. Over dinner the walking conversations continued and we found that we were awakening someone else's dream. The Way may not be for Helen and Stewart but adventure beckoned because our arrival had stirred a sleeping giant.

Why I walk is one of those questions that should be easy to answer but somehow as I grasp for the reason, it fluctuates and eludes before finally disappearing into the shadows. I've read other people's explanations for walking and for some it is the appeal of the challenge, testing one's mettle against the terrain and the weather. In the end it is the endurance of misery and the satisfaction of knowing they are somehow stronger than the rest of us that spurs them on. For others, it is the journey, both internal and external. They seek a type of enlightenment from being closer to nature and living a simpler life.

As I investigate my motivations I realise that I don't feel any need to measure myself against nature because whatever the outcome nature is always the winner. And as for the journey, I enjoy the calm of walking but have never felt anything more.

## *Chapter Sixteen*

I have tried to write this section several times and each time as I feel I am on the verge of illustrating why I walk, the shadows close in and the significance vanishes. So rather than force significance upon it, I believe that we walk for the enjoyment, for the company, for friendship's sake. Perhaps the best reasons of all.

After dinner, we sat down beside the warmth of the fire in the front room. Stewart persuaded us to have a whisky (oh my, the debt that we owe grows by the minute) and we continued to answer questions about the walking we have enjoyed. Nursing the warming whisky I leant over and felt my boots: there's quite a way to go before they meet the specifications printed on the side of the adhesive tin. Meanwhile, James poked around the ashes in the grate and then threw some more coals on the fire and soon it was roaring again.

Suddenly an ember spat out on to the newspaper. My boots, that up until this moment had been lightly grilled, were now getting the full flaming experience. The gentle conversation was brought to an abrupt halt as I rushed to rescue them from the teeth of the fire. Someone threw the burning newspaper into the grate and once the fire was contained I checked over my boots, which along with the dirt and muck now had a black singed area. A first glance suggested that there was some damage to the boot lace eyelets as they are mere loops of material and were most exposed to the flames.

The beer, the meal and the whisky numbed me to the perilous state of my boots and because my eyes were tired and my body weary, I headed off early to bed.

And slept surprisingly soundly.

# FLASHBACK

**August 31, 1979**

The woollen plus twos that I had bought as pukka walking gear from the Scout Shop in Newgate Street were becoming loose and a thick rib of cloth rubbed at my thigh. Slowly and persistently as we walked along Hadrian's Wall and then through Kielder Forest the irritation increased until it became unbearable. Removing my walking trousers in Bellingham youth hostel that evening, I discovered that the top of my left thigh was red raw from contact with the now loose gusset.

We had been allocated bunks in the same room as the irritating lone walker who collected rail tickets. Fortunately he had a spare bandage, which he gladly gave to me. Utilising this bandage and changing into a pair of jeans that up until that moment had been my evening wear got me through the rest of the walk.

He declined to come down to the town with us to eat, preferring to cook his own dinner and probably sing folk songs in the common room. However, we lingered longer than we had anticipated in the pub, (probably because, as Chris has mentioned we actually ate two meals, one Dalesteak, chips and peas did not begin to fill us up). On our return to the hostel we were met on the dark path by an irate hostel manager who had just locked the front door.

The ticket collector anticipated that we may be stranded outside and had left a window open, just in case.

# FLASHBACK

**September 1, 1979**

We always tried to get the odd job that the hostel warden required finished the night before so we could leave earlier, which was just as well as we suspected the warden may have wanted us to clean the toilets as penance for last night.

Through the window of our bunk room we could see that there was a fine misty dampness in the air. It was neither wet, nor dry. We debated whether to wear the nylon waterproofs that keep the rain off but with the unfortunate side effect of creating a heavy warm sweat. In the end I put mine on, while Chris faced the mizzle in his checked shirt.

The six members of 'Wainwrights out' were standing disconsolate at the door of the hostel. As we walked through we could hear a whiney exchange between them about whether or not they could brave this mildly adverse weather.

Truly they were a pathetic bunch.

**The claustrophobic Kielder Forest in 1979**

Mapping:
https://www.wikiloc.com/hiking-trails/pw-14-bellingham-to-cotonshopeburnfoot-97162850

Lonely Northumberland moorland

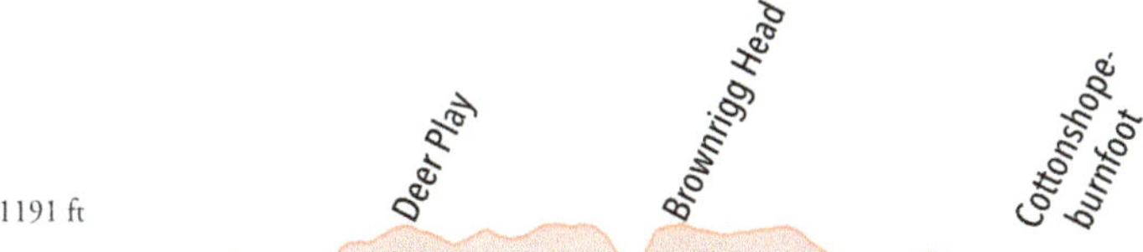


# Chapter 17 - Bellingham to Cottonshopeburnfoot

Total ascent: 27082 ft | Total distance: 231.29 miles

September 11th

**Duncan:** I was gently woken by the dull light of morning creeping around the curtains and I began to ponder the day ahead. It was not a difficult day, a steady tread over the plains of lonely Northumberland moorland and then the forest tracks of Redesdale. As the sky lightened outside, slowly lifting the ambient level in the bedroom, I opened the curtains to survey the sky. The weather looked set to be similar to yesterday with sunshine and clouds.

Then a small niggling issue arose in my mind. It is time to reassess Frances Morris's quote about comfortable shoes because comfort is just one consideration. When I bought my boots I assumed that they would be dependable, robust and have a good grip. Comfort was an added but welcome bonus. Admittedly my boots gripped flagstones really well but on any type of mud they had no purchase at all. To, I would suggest, a dangerous degree.

Now they were falling apart and after only two hundred or so miles of walking which I thought was an unforgivable failing. Although I'd have to admit that my boots were still comfortable, even though the walking no longer was.

I quickly washed, dressed and headed down to the front room to view the semi-cremated remains from the night before. Looking at the positives, the boots were definitely dry and my right boot had negligible damage. My right boot was ready to be glued. My right boot, to paraphrase Peter Cook, was a fine boot for the role.

However the left boot was not fine, not fine at all. Most alarmingly there were some dramatic changes to the laces and eyelets. I took the boots to the utility room and set to work. The heat had caught and charred two of the eyelets. Gingerly I began to remove the brittle lace and it crumbled in my fingers, then despite my gentle touch, one by one the eyelets tore through, rendering them unusable and more distressingly, irreparable. Carefully and cautiously I removed the last of the lace.

I surveyed the remains; there was a full set of four loops on the right side of the lacings but only two on the left, which, looking at the positives again, were at the bottom and the top of the boot. Helen found some spare boot laces and as I drew the thick thread through the remaining fragile loops, I fully expected to tear the fixing. Somehow the remaining loops still had enough integrity to take the lace and tie up.

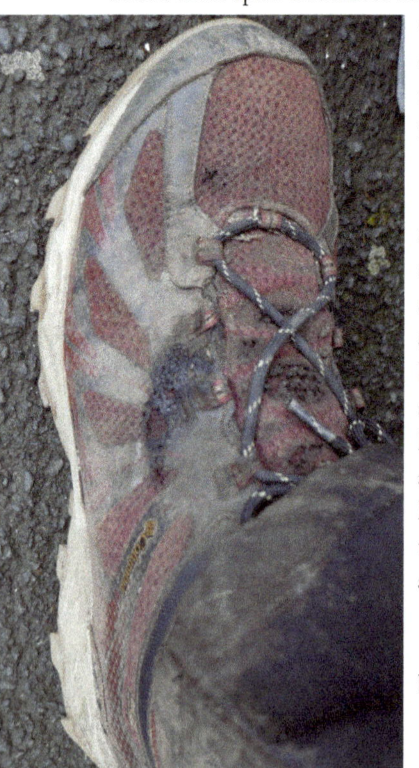

There was hope.

Now for the next stage. Using a matchstick I ran a thin film of sticky adhesive over the gaping sides of my soles. The instructions said that I should leave this for twenty minutes before bringing the surfaces together and for once I followed them to the letter, setting an alarm on my phone and carefully watching over the boots like a mother hen. The alarm went and to my amazement, on contact the sides stuck.

Hard.

I might be able to continue with my boots after all.

**Post repair, fingers crossed …**

Feeling hugely relieved I joined Stewart in the kitchen where he was busy preparing porridge with Chris and Helen in attendance. There was an air of anxious anticipation as both Helen and Stewart were feeling guilty about the state of my boots. I assured them I really didn't believe that anyone was to blame for this, it was just one of those things. Occasionally bad things happen and last night it was my turn. Chris then said, 'If you don't feel your boots can do it, we could stop now' and this comment, coming seemingly from nowhere, almost completely poleaxed me.

Not for a moment had I even begun to entertain the idea of jacking it in. To be honest my thoughts had not gone beyond fixing the boots and I suppose I should have spent some time considering a back-up plan. However that would have meant lying awake worrying. Whereas the reality was that last night when my head hit the pillow, sleep followed immediately. Now I began to wonder what rabbit holes the conversation had fallen into last night after I left. Maybe to Chris, Helen and Stewart I looked dead on my feet.

In reply to Chris, I said, 'No way. We carry on.'

We've come this far, it's time to put the Pennine Way to bed. In my head I was thinking, the idea, the very idea of returning home was unconscionable. I will walk it in my socks if I have to.

The breakfast was ready and so we sat down and this topic of conversation was quickly forgotten. The talk instead was about what Helen and Stewart could do with the little house at the bottom of their garden which was where James and Gina were living until they'd saved enough for a deposit on a home of their own. We talked about Hadrian's Wall, a World Heritage site practically on their doorstep that attracts visitors galore from all over the world. Surely this little house could be converted into ideal accommodation for these travellers as either a b&b or self catering.

Having planted this thought to evict James and Gina, we smiled guiltily as they came in to say goodbye before they left to go to their respective workplaces. Hopefully a few weeks would elapse before they were served notice.

We packed up our bags and loaded up the car before saying a final fond farewell to Haltwhistle. An hour later we were in the picturesque town square of Bellingham and after profusely thanking Stewart and Helen for all the help and wishing them both well for the future, we mooched around for a place to buy some supplies. After the cosseting of the last two days it was time to stand on our own two feet as around us were the last shops or eating places until the end of the Pennine Way.

Chris had ascertained that at the next campsite they had a kettle and a microwave oven and they also kindly offered us coffee and milk. So in the tiny supermarket we were trying to choose things that were not too heavy, that we could cook using the available options and might fill us up. After some debate we bought some sandwiches and cold coffee for lunch. For dinner, a pre-packed burger; for breakfast tomorrow some microwaveable bacon muffins and pots of porridge. For dessert, a large bunch of bananas and a bag full of clementines.

We took our bounty outside and distributed it among our packs. Despite the mountainous quantities of food, we knew deep down that this would not be enough, especially as we were not entirely confident about crossing the Cheviots in one walking day. We stoically believed that we were prepared for a little hunger.

The day's walk was weirdly ordinary. An average amount of mileage and a slightly below average amount of climbing across featureless moor and through plantation forest. It was an interstitial day, a dour necessity in order to reach the Cheviot Hills but lacking in almost any remarkable features. The Pennine Way was holding up a mirror to itself as, it could be argued, there is a similar rural gap between the end of the Dark Peak at Blackstone Edge and the beginning of limestone country at Malham. The main difference being that the Northumberland countryside is wild, remote and empty.

The path struggled out of the valley of the North Tyne, up through some rough farmland before reaching open moorland. The wind blew hard and fast and although the views were extensive there was little to catch and even less to delight the eye. On a boggy path, we reached the broad flat heights of Deer Play, a delightful name for yet more featureless moorland where innocent grouse hid amongst the

**Deer Play 2019**

**Deer Play 1979**
**That's a fellow walker staring with a look of existential despair**
**Chris with his head in his hands is probably wishing**
**he'd worn his waterproofs**

bedraggled heather, unaware that the calendar had ticked around and soon the shooting butts would be filled with intrepid hunters. We sat for a few moments and watched as the heather was combed one way and then another by the fierce sweeping wind.

In the far distance we could see a lone walker making his way to the next high point, Lord's Shaw. We followed the lie of a path that seemed to head in this direction only to find after nearly half a mile that it gradually turned away. There was no doubt that we had followed the wrong path. Yet again Wikiloc's audible 'weep, weep' warning function failed to alert us.

We decided to cut across to where we believed the Pennine Way to be on the other side of a dip and were swiftly mired in a serious bit of blanket bog. What we should have done here was turn around and retrace our steps until we came across the right path. Instead we slowly picked our way across the sedges that became more and more infiltrated with sphagnum moss until we finally hit the flagstone path.

I have found that if a bog is mainly sedge, then it is generally passable. Once sphagnum moss becomes involved, it is time to proceed with caution because it can hold up to twenty six times its weight in water so should probably be best thought of as neon green water, and if that sphagnum has even a hint of open water, turn back. It is better to retreat, rather than break through the fragile skin of sphagnum and sink into a stinking deep morass.

From the top of Lord's Shaw - apparently 'Shaw' refers to woodland, of which there was none visible because it was just another mound of

**Bog (with flagstones) - it looks harmless**

barren moorland - we could see a small tarmac road. Here the Pennine Way diverts from its original route which used to follow this road to Byrness. The Northern Area of the Ramblers' Association petitioned the original designers of the Pennine Way to use some other existing rights of way which included yet more arduous bog. Most of the route they proposed was rejected as it avoided Byrness. This would have made the last section of the Way a two or even three day journey from Bellingham to Kirk Yetholm, without the possibility of accommodation or shops and therefore for heroes only.

However a part of their route had been adopted and so we have the Northern Area of the Ramblers' Association to thank for the next few miles of bog where we could enjoy the possibility of dipping our toes, knees and for a few lucky walkers, thighs through the neon green carpet of sphagnum moss.

At a gateway after Padon Hill, we came across Simon and the couple who had led us the wrong way yesterday. They were eating their lunch in the sunshine, while sheltering from the wind. We stopped too and the conversation turned to tomorrow and the Cheviot Hills.

It was easy for them, they had their accommodation booked. Chris tells them that he spoke to owners of the same place about putting up our tent in their garden and booking an evening meal for tonight but the owners were not interested. They were fully booked and could not possibly fit us in, whenever we were arriving. Nor could they, or would they, put out another two chairs at the table and feed us. Making money, being enterprising, or just helping fellow human beings - other than those who have booked long ahead - it seemed was not their main concern (and we were not the first to observe this trait, although there are new owners now I am told).

Instead we were staying at the campsite and after seeing the 'Hobbit Hole' that the young couple used in Dufton, we had booked a 'pod'. For a few pounds more we had the luxury of a wooden hut, with heating and electricity, so we could charge up the technology.

'And what about tomorrow?' the others asked.

Simon and the couple have booked the next two nights in the b&b in Byrness. After about seventeen miles walking across the Cheviots they will descend a mile or so into a lonely valley from where they will be picked up by a Land Rover and return to Byrness for a hot shower, food and a warm bed.

We didn't have anything booked for tomorrow, nor did we have an absolute plan. There were some options, all of which would be desperately unappealing to our fellow walkers, so rather than discuss them, I replied with a non-committal, 'We'll see'.

This was not the answer that they were expecting and they all expressed astonishment that we would countenance attempting the Cheviots without a fully fledged plan. Personally I didn't want to discuss it as none of the options that we were about to face tomorrow were very attractive, so rather than debate it I remained silent.

They ate the last of their food and headed off, leaving us in this sheltered spot to our lunch. This may be a good moment to avoid talking about tomorrow and talk about piccalilli instead.

Sometime last evening at Helen and Stewart's the conversation stumbled over this piquant condiment and I was outed as someone who had recently made some. Chris had commented on the deliciousness of the product and they were keen to find out more.

Now, shop bought piccalilli, like lemon curd, can be terribly disappointing. I have heard of some supermarket brands being vaguely palatable, though in my experience it is a ghastly yellow gloop. The exceptions come at Christmas time when garden centres and delicatessens are filled with various artisan-style piccalillis which can be very tasty, if expensive.

The year before at a gathering at Jerome's along with some cheese and bread he produced a piccalilli that had been made by his next door neighbour. It was delicious and I wanted to know more but by the next day I failed to remember much of the details, so instead I went to the internet and finally after a bit of home experimentation designed the recipe overleaf.

***Piccalilli (2019)***

*Half a large cauliflower*
*3 small onions*
*1 red or green pepper*
*1 large carrot*
*250g runner beans*
*1 large gherkin (pickled)*
*1 pack baby sweetcorn*
*2 cloves of garlic*
*300ml cider vinegar (Aspall's organic if possible)*
*150g demerara sugar*
*300ml water*
*2 teaspoons of dried ginger (or fresh ginger, grated or sliced)*
*2 teaspoons of turmeric or a generous pinch of saffron*
*2 teaspoons of coriander powder (or seeds if preferred)*
*3 teaspoons of Dijon mustard*
*1 teaspoon of Encona hot chilli sauce (or equivalent)*
*4 tablespoons of cornflour*
*5 tablespoons of cooking salt*
*Several sterilised jars for approx 1.5kg.*

***Method***

***Day 1***

*Chop and slice veg, except the gherkin. Slice the veg up so it won't fall off an open sandwich, see picture.*
*Place it all in a salad spinner (if available) and then place the spinner in a large bowl.*
*Salt the vegetables generously with four or five tablespoons of cooking salt.*
*Cover with an old shower cap or cling film.*
*Leave in a cool dark place for a day.*

***Day 2***
*Rinse the veg thoroughly in running water for five minutes.*
*Spin the veg to get it dry. Or leave for an hour.*
*Put the vinegar and water in a large pan, add the ginger, turmeric or saffron and coriander. Bring to the boil and then let simmer.*
*Add the vegetables and mustard and simmer for five minutes.*
*Add the chilli and sugar and cook for a further 2 minutes.*
*Add the chopped gherkin. Stir and mix.*
*Add four tablespoons of cornflour to a couple of tablespoons of cold water then slowly stir in until glossy.*
*Put in sterile jars for a minimum of four weeks.*

This recipe produced the piccalilli in the photograph. The downside is that it has to be made over two days and left for a month before eating. I understand that some people might regard these as onerous conditions especially when it is possible to pop into a garden centre and buy a jar, however I promise you, it is worth the wait.

Back to the Way and we were still munching sandwiches and sipping cold coffee as we watched Simon and the couple labour up Brownrigg Head. Following a few moments later we found the sudden steepness a bit of shock after the gently undulating moors. The top was reached after a short scramble on slippery mud and from here (unless the bog-ridden unofficial alternative of the Northern Area of the Ramblers Association is followed, and by this stage no one in their right mind wants any more of this stuff), it was mainly downhill on a dirt road through the unremarkable Redesdale Forest.

This is the last major forest on the route and yet another plantation of Sitka spruce. I cast my mind back to the woodland that we have walked through and it was rare indeed to spend any time amongst deciduous trees. In fact, beyond the odd valley bottom, I cannot find any trace of it in my memory. I find it hard to believe that no remnant of ancient woodland seemed to exist along the whole length of the Pennine Way.

***Russula emetica* at the edge of the forest, not a wise addition to the menu as it's a bit of a 'sickener'**

I wouldn't argue that the landscape be returned wholesale to its previous state, more that some small part of it could be, if only to allow space for the more endangered indigenous species to thrive. Admittedly Kielder is a stronghold for the red squirrel in England and is also famous for having a nesting pair of osprey. I also understand that the Forestry Commission has begun a project to grow strips of native trees with the aim of offering safe passage for fauna. Maybe this is the start of the answer but what it should not be is merely a facade behind which it is business as usual.

Byrness had shrunk since we were last there. The youth hostel was long gone. The cafe and hotel had closed. There were no shops and the accommodation options were extremely limited. Both ends of the Pennine Way have these very stark options. Crowden, the only sensible stopping point after Edale at the beginning of the Way was also surprisingly lacking in facilities. The problem can be solved either by carrying supplies and tents, or the application of money to book a taxi to places nearby. Byrness it should be noted, is not near anywhere though.

We were staying at the Border Forest Campsite which was just beside the Pennine Way. A traipse past neat ranks of light green static homes led us to the main office where they handed over the key to the pod. Turning back we bumped into Robin, the American walker, emerging towel around waist from the shower block. Again he had been here for hours and he was anxious to return to his tent as he was a little damp.

**Pale green holiday homes, probably similar to the skin colour of anyone who's eaten a 'vomiting fungus'**

We located our pod which was new, warm and toasty because it had basked in the afternoon sun. The interior was almost completely bare, except for a heater and some electrical wall plugs. This allowed us some feeling of virtue for carrying our sleeping pads and bags the entire length of the Pennine Way as they were now pressed into service once more.

I took off my boots and inspected the repair. The glue, sadly, had not held the sides together, though the insides remained dry and the soles were not gaping and full of detritus, unlike yesterday. These boots only have to hold out over the Cheviots and then retirement beckons. Surely they can do that.

I popped back to the shower block and luxuriated in a spacious cubicle. Unusually there was even enough room to avoid my evening clothes being doused by water.

Dotted around the toilet block were numerous handwritten notices, which is never a good sign. There was the unusual, 'Don't put bleach down the loo'. Not a thought that would immediately have occurred to me, as I've never taken bleach on a long distance walk. Mobile home dwellers, it seems have other ideas.

Then there was 'Keep your dog under control'. One of those signs which I think we can agree comes under the category of common sense as 'let your dog run wild' is nobody's idea of a good time.

Then there was 'No refunds for midges' and I am sure that you can make up your own jokes here. Covertly the sign was a warning that 'here be the voracious man-eating insects of northern Britain' and us hardy souls staying at the Border Forest campsite had better man-up or move on.

Or scuttle back to the pod and cover myself with Smidge (other insect repellent brands are available, but when it comes to midges they're just not as effective).

It was early but the thought of cooking while fighting off midges led us to the kitchen, which had yet more strident handwritten signs. Ripping a burger out of its packaging, I placed it on one of the plastic plates that had been left for our use and stuck it in the microwave. The slowly revolving plate promptly shattered. Oops. Down to one plate, I put the next burger in using the packaging that came with it which, in the furnace of the microwave, distorted and threatened to melt in an alarming manner. Despite this cooking fiasco we rescued and consumed the food and then quickly wished that we hadn't. It was truly vile. Whose idea was this? Mine, unfortunately.

We made a coffee and retreated to the pod before the midges made an entrance. There was a knock on our door and Robin had come over to tell us he is leaving at 6.00 am tomorrow with the intention of finishing that evening, especially as he had seen the weather forecast which promised that along with the constant wind, there would be rain, turning heavy in the afternoon. Then he mentioned that he had bumped into Rob and his wife earlier that day and we were surprised. Surely Rob should be finished by now as his schedule had him accelerating away from us after we last saw him in Hawes?

Although we had barely met Robin, it was sad to say goodbye but he was off to bed early to be ready for tomorrow. With the news that Rob was nearby and mobile we tried to contact him using an email address that he'd given us. We would like to see him again so that we could exchange tales and indeed find out why he was still here. Especially if his wife was able to pick us up in their car and take us on a magic carpet ride to a place with a convivial atmosphere, that provided beer and pork scratchings.

The message sent, we awaited a reply and when finally an hour or so later I looked at my phone I realised that although a reply had come and we could have crossed paths, my phone had failed to notify me. So that window had now closed.

Ever since walking over Wain Rigg my phone had not worked properly. The dampness that day must have got to it. We had dropped into a hollow to cross a stream when suddenly my phone came to life at full volume. The radio app was somehow selected and a reporter was shouting out of my pocket 'there are incredible scenes here in the House of Commons', giving a picture of the events that occurred just after the vote to prorogue Parliament. Maybe the whole fabric of space-time was affected at that moment and certainly my phone took the brunt of it as almost no feature had worked properly since then.

The midges had yet to make an appearance, so for a short while I sat outside at the trestle table resetting my phone. I glanced up as a dog walker passed by and the hound looked back at me. I've never seen such a look of utter existential despair on any animal's face. It was as if the dog had been found out of control pouring a bottle of bleach down one of the toilets and was now being taken on a punishment walk to the place of midges. The poor mutt gazed at me with pleading eyes for mercy.

There was an outside lamp on our pod which illuminated the porch and around it I could already see a dancing cloud of insects. Discretion being the better part and all that, I retreated inside and turned the light off. It was still early, although dusk was settling in. We lay down on our sleeping pads and listened to some radio comedies before calling it a night.

Later on, my bladder succumbed to that full feeling and I had no choice but to head off to the distant facilities. It was a dark starlit night. This is one of the few dark sky areas in the United Kingdom and fearless stargazers, once their eyes acclimatise, can marvel at such natural wonders as the Milky Way.

My eyes were fixed firmly on the blue-white light emanating from the small toilet block nearby. I dashed across and once inside I was confronted by yet another sign that read: 'Keep the door closed so Mr Midge and his friends don't come in and play'. Mr Midge was not aware that his presence was unwelcome as he and his numerous friends had gatecrashed the brightly lit toilet. Many hundreds of the wee beasties were swinging unhappily on a spiders web that covered the overhead light panel. After a rapid toilet stop I returned unbitten (thank you Smidge) to the warm pod, to sleep.

Which would have been more successful if my inflatable pillow had not developed a slow leak.

**Redesdale Forest, 1979**

Mapping:
https://www.wikiloc.com/hiking-trails/pw-15-byrness-red-cribbs-41186840

Mapping:
https://www.wikiloc.com/hiking-trails/pw-15-1-red-cribbs-to-mounthooly-41203280

**Cheviot mania**
**A rare delusional state seen in Pennine Way walkers who believe that as they've managed to make it this far, how much harder can it be? Those walkers (north-southers) who go in the opposite direction often experience Kinder Downfall**

First Refuge
Windy Gyle
Red Cribbs
Mountholy

2449 ft

# Chapter 18 - Cottonshopeburnfoot to Mounthooly

663 ft 20.76 mi

Total ascent: 30245 ft Total distance: 252.05 miles

September 12th

**Chris:** Waking up after an excellent night's sleep in the pod, we knew that we would definitely complete the Pennine Way for the second time. And with that knowledge, for me, came the first pangs of nostalgia. The end was nigh; in a couple of days we'd be back home and I was already missing waking up to the Pennine morning, surrounded by hills and uplifted by the prospect of setting out on another day in this wonderful landscape.

As had become our habit, we didn't leap to a supercharged start, unlike Robin we imagined, who was probably already long gone. Instead we enjoyed the warmth of our sleeping bags (for once) and chose not to tackle the elephant in the pod: although we had vaguely discussed plans for crossing the Cheviots, we had no firm decision on a strategy. Byrness to Kirk Yetholm, the last day for some, is tackled by most over two days. It is twenty eight miles: that would be a

**The pod at Border Forest: quite a bit better than a tent**

challenging distance in good conditions on the flat, but after the fortnight we'd just had we weren't expecting 'good' conditions and with a total climb of nearly four thousand feet it is certainly not flat.

The Border Forest Holiday Park where our pod was is strictly speaking not in Byrness, but is encountered bang on the path about a mile short of Byrness, at the admirably named Cottonshopeburnfoot. It is a well-appointed site, clean with good showers and a kitchen for campers' use close to the pods. The Park's residents would normally be mostly caravan dwellers but on this morning, presumably because the school holidays had ended, the place seemed deserted and not a little desolate. We both wondered what might attract people to holiday here.

Nevertheless it had worked out well for us, the only other option in Byrness, the Forest View Walkers Inn, being fully booked. A small hotel, the Walkers Inn occupies the building which in 1979 was the youth hostel in which we'd stayed. I had hoped that we'd be able to stay in the hostel this time, but had been disappointed to find that sometime in the intervening years the YHA had closed it. If the Walkers Inn had had vacancies, Duncan and I might have considered availing ourselves of it and its transport options. It is worth noting though, if you happen to be planning your own attempt, that this option will deliver you to Kirk Yetholm late in the day, and getting out of the village will be difficult.

Anyway, back to the elephant. Like this time, our strategy for the final stage forty years ago was similarly vague. We'd known that there was a bothy - actually a re-purposed railway goods wagon - at about eighteen miles and that if necessary we could probably overnight in that. The final seven miles could be done the following morning allowing a lunchtime arrival at Kirk Yetholm. It worked out very well: the goods wagon, positioned at a place labelled on the OS as Red Cribbs was spacious and had benches around the inside of it which were wide enough to lie on, which is exactly what we did. Perhaps surprisingly, we were able to enjoy a decent night's sleep.

Although it had been fairly gloomy and at times misty early in the day, later it became clearer and intermittent sunshine brightened up the trek. The evening was warm and properly sunny and we scrambled down into the very steep sided valley immediately to the north to get water for cooking. All things considered it had worked out very well and I think in the back of our minds was the idea that we would just do the same this time. We knew that there was still a shelter at Red Cribbs, though we knew also that it wasn't the same one and there was a slight worry in my mind that the more modern shed might be a less accommodating venue.

There was an alternative which we didn't have before: the Mounthooly Bunkhouse. Just in case we needed it, I had contacted the proprietor Charlene before leaving home and knew that if necessary, we'd be able to stay in the bunkhouse. However, due to its location some distance off the route and indeed off the hills, I have to say I viewed it as a last resort.

There was also a time constraint that informed our thinking, in that we needed to be at Kirk Yetholm at lunchtime on Day 16. After we bade farewell to Helen and Stewart in Bellingham they had decided that, as if they hadn't done enough for us, they would drive to Kirk Yetholm, meet us at the Border Hotel for a celebratory lunch and then drive us to Newcastle station, a mere hundred and sixty mile round trip. Their intention was revealed to us in a text from James, who also indicated that there would be no debate about it – this is what would be happening. Apart from being immensely kind, this was incredibly helpful because making the journey by public transport would have been tedious and very time consuming, if my reading of the bus timetables was correct.

We avoided having to use public transport forty years ago too. Then, I had persuaded my brother (Bernard, remember him in Hebden Bridge?) to collect us from Kirk Yetholm and take us back to his place in Carlisle, from where we could make our way back to London. In those pre-mobile phone days we couldn't confirm our arrival at the

Border Hotel until we were actually there, so by the time he arrived we'd had our free pint of beer and several we had to pay for, heard from the landlord what a twat that John Noakes was, had something to eat, and were working our way along the optics in celebration of our great achievement. We were I think it's fair to say, three sheets to the wind when he found us.

So, when we eventually bade farewell to the pod, I think the assumption was that the last two days would pretty well match the last two in 1979, and I think we were both pretty relaxed about that. Not quite so relaxed about the fairly small amount of food we had with us this time – bananas and a few biscuits – but we'd had a bowl of microwave porridge and a fairly disgusting 'muffin' and figured we'd be ok. Not so relaxed either about how the weather might turn out: the sky was heavily overcast, not at all promising. It was fairly cold and surprise surprise, windy.

For the first mile though we were fairly sheltered as the path passed

**A pleasant forest track along the River Rede**

along a pleasant forest track alongside the river Rede to Byrness, before crossing the last sign of civilisation for many miles, the A68. The first climb arrived almost immediately on the other side of the road and by the time we reached the top of Byrness Hill the rain had started, though fairly lightly at first. However, as I stopped to take a photograph of the ominous cloud to the north and What'sApp it to the family to fill them in on this morning's prospects, it was obvious to us that they were not good. The rain gear went on, and would not be coming off anytime soon.

The path across the Cheviots mostly follows the England/Scotland border which we first hit after about four miles of more or less continuous climb. There is actually a fence running the whole way along the border over these hills. Apart from a couple of forays, the Pennine Way stays largely in England and it won't be until tomorrow that we will leave England permanently. It's a desolate landscape, not enhanced by the conditions which further deteriorated as we trudged

**Plenty of signs for the army but none to be seen anywhere**

**On the path to Chew Green**

over the wet moorland towards the first staging post, the Roman fort at Chew Green. The Romans must have loved being posted here! We didn't actually make it to the fort though because about a mile or so before it, an alternative track heading off to the left presented itself. Checking the map, we saw that this option would allow us to cut off the dog-leg in the main path that took in Chew Green. It is worth going to see the remains – once – so having done that in 1979 and given the conditions, we took the opportunity today to cut out a bit of mileage.

It has been observed previously that rainy, windswept conditions such as we were walking in are not conducive to chat, so inevitably thoughts once again turned to home. I'd kept in regular contact with Mag, whose siblings had all now returned home. The funeral was set for exactly a week's time and all the planning seemed to be complete, but after a conversation I'd had with her on the morning we left Helen and Stewart for the second time, I was feeling anxious about not being with her. It had become evident that she thought we'd be home today,

**Conditions had been better in '79**

not tomorrow and the disappointment in her voice when she realised went through me like a bolt of lightning. I instantly felt the need to be with her. I found Duncan in our hosts' utility room attempting to repair his boots which were not just coming apart at the seams, but were now extensively fire damaged too, and put it to him that we could go home if he felt his boot problem was insurmountable. I think I may have meant that *I* needed to go home without wanting to accept 'blame' for us giving up, so no wonder he found my suggestion incomprehensible. In retrospect I find it incomprehensible too, but it seems that my ability to act rationally had temporarily deserted me. Duncan said if necessary he'd find a shop and buy new boots, and his 'No way am I stopping now' brought me to my senses. Of course not even Mag would want me to stop so close to the end, so now here we were 'enjoying' the final stage.

Past the Roman remains the unpleasantly boggy path continued initially with the fence but soon arced away from it and the route-finding assistance it provided was lost. The route is however, by and large, fairly obvious and easy to follow; probably a good thing in terms of the young man we encountered who was on a north-south attempt with no form of mapping at all! He told us that we had more bog to endure which wasn't well received but added the more than welcome news that eventually we would meet flagstones. Sploshing along, we looked forward to that!

Perhaps surprisingly there are a number of footpaths here, to the west of the Way and running down into the Coquet valley, through which a small access road winds its way to Chew Green. The paths converge on a mountain rescue hut, the next landmark that presented itself to us.

Duncan and I have never really been ones for 'resting': we'll stop occasionally to take in a view or discuss a point of interest but generally we prefer to just keep going. Had we wanted to take a few moments out of the rain at the shelter however, we'd have been disappointed as we found it full of Duke of Edinburgh's award students, the first we'd seen since the first couple of days. It didn't look as though they were particularly enjoying their day, and their teacher confirmed as much. As Duncan noted, this must be some kind of aversion therapy: it's hard to imagine the youngsters developing a love of hill walking from what they were going through.

**Duncan:** While I did feel sympathy for those Duke of Edinburgh students having to endure this appalling weather, I was by this stage feeling much more sorry for myself. My left boot had decided to stop pretending to be waterproof before we had even reached the top of Byrness Hill and by the time we had met the young man who was walking the Way without maps both my boots were letting in water. They were not just damp but could have doubled as a matching pair of novelty kitchen colanders.

I had so looked forward to walking over the Cheviots. It was one of my favourite days of the first walk and my memories are of a bleak and barren landscape of quiet solitude. Today my thoughts were filled with wretchedness, the only thing that kept me going was the realisation that the time and miles must pass and this will finish. My mind swirled with remarks and comments wrought from the ghastly motivational speeches of a hundred or more commercial conferences, which I had filmed for various clients. Words of significance and substance, like resilience and persistence. Although I despised the source of these slogans and catchphrases, I formed a mantra to convince myself that this ordeal will end. It was my final protection as the rain and wind closed in on us.

**Chris:** By this time we'd covered about nine miles, so were roughly half way to where we thought the day might end. Wishing the teachers luck in tempting their charges out of the shelter, we headed off, aiming for the top of Windy Gyle, some six hundred feet of ascent ahead.

The very name Windy Gyle conjures a lonely, bleak and well, windswept place, and it certainly was all of those things on this day. It is a broad, flattish hill which sits in the middle of the Cheviots and from it we would have had a fantastic panoramic view across the rest of the range forty years ago. Not today, alas. I have since decided that I'd really like to come here again on a good day. Cars might play a bigger role in that journey! Today though, things being as they were, it was a case of head down, no nonsense, mindless walking and I'm not sure either of us even clocked that we'd passed over the summit.

We now began the biggest climb of the stage, cruelly positioned fairly late in the day at about fifteen miles. From King's Seat to Cairn Hill is about six hundred and fifty feet of steady ascent but in these conditions it was a real test. As the young north-souther had described, there were flagstones, which we greeted gratefully when they appeared, but most of the time they were set lower than the surrounding ground, creating channels which were being turned into fast flowing rivers by the vast amount of water falling from the sky.

After what by now had been several hours of persistent heavy rain, I was once again soaked to the skin, but this time felt worse than before: I was very cold and it felt like the end was further away than it

**At least there were flagstones**

had been at any other time. My feet were cold and wet from water getting into my boots through the top, but at least they weren't actually leaking. I felt for Duncan whose boots appeared to be simply falling apart, shipping gallons of water. It seemed they'd also lost all vestige of grip as he slipped and slid and fell heavily on several occasions. He was behind me for a while – it was single file traffic here – and I stopped frequently to be sure we were keeping close together. After one particularly heavy fall he seemed pretty shaken up and he certainly didn't look on top of his game. The constant struggle to prevent further calamity was draining him of energy and I suggested that a banana consumed now might be helpful so we took a breather, had a drink and expressed opinions about how effing awful this was before pressing on to the top of Cairn Hill.

The summit of Cairn Hill offers walkers two options: turn left and follow the main Pennine Way route or turn right and head off on a short, there-and-back visit to the summit of the Cheviot. Wainwright derides this detour to what he describes as the 'highest but least attractive of the border peaks' and suggests you 'do it if you must' but that you shouldn't expect to enjoy it. Some misguided sense of completeness (which we don't have) is required to do things like that and in any case, only a fool would do it in the conditions we were experiencing.

We therefore took the left turn to head to the next landmark, Auchope cairn, only a fairly short distance away but invisible in the impenetrable grey. On a good day there is no doubt that we'd be able to see exactly where we were headed, but despite the flagstones we managed to get off the path. While we indulged in some wandering back and forth I took a leaf out of Duncan's book and fell fairly spectacularly when my feet slid from under me. Landing heavily and face down in soggy peat, I laid for more than a few moments considering the pain coming from one knee and the elbow that had taken most of the impact, before struggling uneasily to my feet. Duncan, now ahead of me knew nothing of this and was disappearing into the gloom having reconnected with the path. Hoping not to lose sight of him I eventually followed as quickly as was safe, and caught up at Auchope cairn. From there we were both relieved at last to see the hut that might provide the night's accommodation, not too far away at the top of another, though mercifully modest, climb.

Cheered by the opportunity to be able to get out of these vile conditions at last we strode toward the shelter, but as we approached, the disappointment was palpable as our doubts about it as a venue for the night were confirmed. It was much smaller than the previous goods wagon bothy, and stepping inside we immediately knew we couldn't stay there. The interior seemed tiny: we would have had to sleep sitting up as the benches were so small, but much worse was the realisation that after only a couple of minutes we were absolutely freezing. We probably would never have properly dried out and might have perished in the meantime.

Despite our tiredness I was becoming reconciled to continuing on to Mounthooly after all. A quick discussion confirmed our agreement

**Peering into College Valley**

that the extra couple of miles was the only option. As it happened there was a flyer on the shelter wall advertising the bunkhouse so Duncan called the number before we left the shelter. An answering machine responded, then we were called back, but a weak signal prevented any actual conversation so we headed off anyway.

The bunkhouse is in the valley of College Burn which we could look straight into on leaving the shelter. The valley ran due north from Red Cribbs and looking down into it our eyes were led to the edge of the Cheviot Hills and a green landscape beyond which was bathed in sunshine. Getting down there seemed even more of a good idea, so no more than a few hundred yards beyond the shelter we turned off and headed down the steep path into the valley. The ground was initially wet, but descent was rapid and by the time we hit a good track our spirits were much raised: it had stopped raining for the first time in hours and the prospects for soon being clean and warm were very good.

Arriving at Mounthooly, at first we couldn't find a way in or indeed any signs of life. Maybe the abortive call back we'd received on top of the hill was proprietor Charlene telling us she was closed. We found that the drying room was open and warm and just as we'd decided that we'd sleep in there if necessary, the delightful Charlene showed up. We were introduced to the bunkhouse, of which we were the only guests, save a trio of blokes who were working in the area and who had their own room. As in Horton therefore, we had the large dormitory to ourselves.

Charlene asked if we had any food and somewhat embarrassedly, sounding like a pair of twerps who'd tackled the Cheviots stupidly unprepared, we admitted we hadn't. She offered to rustle up 'a ham roll or something?' – and left saying she'd be back soon. Meanwhile we chose and made up our bunks and showered, before reconvening in the kitchen to find two huge ham rolls and two tins of chicken

**The unassuming but welcoming Mounthooly bunkhouse**

soup. Simple fare, but it really hit the spot and we couldn't have been more grateful.

Having eaten, we reflected on the day. It had been awful by any standards – even the locals, in the shape of Charlene's husband who dropped in to say hello, agreed that it had been pretty bad on top. Still, it was over, another memory and tale to tell. With luck, tomorrow would be a better day, with weather in keeping with our glorious arrival into Kirk Yetholm.

We slept well…

The view from Windy Gyle in '79
Cocklawfoot farm is caught by a sunbeam
The Cheviot is the peak on the right

# FLASHBACK

**September 3, 1979**

Outside the sun rose and clouds skidded over the Cheviot Hills. Inside the railway goods van, which had been pressed into service as a mountain rescue hut above Red Cribbs, we were woken by a shaft of light which slowly formed into a remarkable scene. A knot hole in the wood was acting as a perfect *camera obscura*, projecting onto the wooden slats opposite an upside down panoramic view of College Valley to the north east and the sun rising above it.

I turned on the transistor radio, my one luxury item and the sound of Edwin Starr belting out 'Happy Radio' filled the wagon.

It was going to be a good day.

**Top: the railway goods van**
**Opposite: a good morning at Red Cribbs**

# FLASHBACK

**Sometime in late 2000**

**Duncan:** I used to work with Stewart, a sound recordist, whose wife was an executive at Universal Music. She offered me the job of filming their artists' publicity interviews, rather than continuing to use the hard-bitten broadcast news crews who apparently treated the talent with some contempt. Having accepted the challenge I quickly learnt that once in the filming room no one was interested in my opinion and if I got the job done with the minimum of fuss, then everyone was happy.

We were packaging interviews for MTV and driving into central London and setting up in a posh hotel room became a regular gig. At the time I got an autograph book so I could collect these coveted items for my daughter.

One particular interview was with rising star Samantha Mumba. She had just had a run of hit singles and was about to leave to go to Hollywood where she had a starring role in a movie of HG Wells's 'The Time Machine'. I remember her especially because she was very young and still enjoying that happy moment of innocence before the whirlwind of fame messed with her worldview. She was also very pretty and the camera adored her face, so much so that with a little gentle lighting, her beauty was dazzling.

There was a break in filming - someone must have been late for one of the run of interviews, so unusually we all went off together to the coffee lounge area in this five star hotel (normally the crew would be left behind to sit in the room, guarding the equipment). Samantha Mumba's entourage sat noisily down, taking up a large corner and there was one other person in the room, an old guy sitting at a table, nursing a coffee and reading through some notes while checking his phone and his watch.

One of the execs from Polydor Records leaned across the table and quietly said,

'You know who that is, don't you?'

Shyly Samantha went across and awkwardly introduced herself. Then she remembered that her mum was a big fan so she took out her phone to tell her where she was and who she was with, before handing the phone over to Edwin Starr so that he could say hello. Edwin handled the moment with tremendous style and had a generous conversation with both Samantha and her mother.

Once they had finished I remembered my autograph book. I fished it out from my bag and went over to say… suddenly I was not entirely sure what I wanted to say. I wanted to tell him about the Pennine Way and the fact that his single 'Happy Radio' had set the tone for the last day. The stunning walking bass-line, his stirring voice, with all the power of his first hit single 'War'. It picked me up and took me over the line. I bought the single when I got home. I had even, a few years later, included it on a compilation cassette entitled 'My Top Twelve' after the Radio 1 show of the same name. Now I wished I could've rushed home and brought back this piece of vinyl, to have him sign this precious memento.

Instead, tongue tied and bumbling, I stumbled through some badly thought out sentences about the Pennine Way and 'Happy Radio' which probably made very little sense to him. Then I was about to say something along the lines of 'it just being a silly little pop song but it meant the world to me' when something inside warned me that he probably wouldn't appreciate that characterisation. Because the reality of being a genuinely creative person is that it takes unbelievable effort to be effortless - whatever the end product.

Somehow I managed to avoid any major offence and return with his autograph.

Mapping:
https://www.wikiloc.com/hiking-trails/pw-16-mounthooly-kirk-yetholm-41207182

The autograph and opposite inside the bunkhouse

1815 ft

Black Hag

Burnhead Farm

Last Hill

Kirk Yetholm

# Chapter 19 - Mounthooly to Kirk Yetholm

536 ft

6.61 mi

Total ascent: 31160 ft

258.66 miles

September 13th

**Duncan:** The sound of music interspersed with the chink of cooking utensils and jovial conversation percolated up from the kitchen into the bunk room above. The three other residents who we'd been informed were working on a moorland regeneration project were engaged in preparations for breakfast. I turned over in bed to glance at the time on my phone. It was early, 6.00 am, so closing my eyes I drifted back into a shallow sleep. Sometime later fierce sunlight slanted in through the attic window, insisting that the morning was here. I sensed movement from Chris's bunk and we began the day.

## *Chapter Nineteen*

Downstairs in the kitchen there was no sign of the previous occupants. Everything was back in its place, except that on one of the kitchen surfaces there was a loaf of bread, butter, some coffee powder, milk and a note:

*I have to take the children to school and I do not expect to be back until 09.30. Here is the invoice for your stay. Please place the money through the letterbox to the bungalow.*

*I have left you some bread, coffee and milk.*

*Charlene*

With this magnificent offering our meagre breakfast had been upgraded to mashed banana on toast. We then discovered that we had more bananas than we thought, meaning there were double helpings which were washed down with a couple of cups of coffee. At this moment life was unexpectedly, uncommonly, good.

Glancing at the invoice I noticed that Charlene hadn't charged us for any of the food that she'd given us. Well that was not going to happen. I mean money may not be everything for this saint in human form but there was no way that she'd be left out of pocket on our account.

Breakfast finished and the dishes cleared, we wandered outside into the bright warm sunshine and then checked out our clothes and boots in the drying room. Almost everything was dry but my socks were still damp so they got an extra tumble in the drier. My boots, which yesterday acted as conduits for every molecule of water on top of the Cheviots may never recover, and could probably best be described as irredeemably sodden.

I shuddered at the memory of yesterday. The boots losing their waterproofness in the morning was just the beginning of my misery as their other major failing came to the fore in the afternoon. The sheer wetness caused me to slip repeatedly. Each time I fell more heavily but rather like a boxer who is trying to show that the fall was nothing, I was quickly on my feet. On the fourth occasion it was different. As we were coming down towards Auchope cairn, I tried to avoid slipping on the peat by crossing some large boulders, thinking that my boots would grip the rocky surface like the flagstones. Suddenly I went flying and landed heavily on a stone. The wind was completely taken out of me and I lay there for a few moments assessing the damage. I could feel that my strength was ebbing away and the only thing that got me back on my feet was the knowledge that the mountain rescue hut was only a mile or two ahead, although we couldn't see more than thirty yards in any direction due to the low cloud.

**A bump on the ridge**

Today it was a cloudless blue sky day. To the south, at the head of the valley, the lonely mountain rescue hut that we walked down from yesterday appeared as a tiny bump on the ridge. It was strange to think that last evening when we made the difficult decision to leave the refuge, we walked north out of Scotland and returned to England as College Valley is in Northumberland. I was fearful as we left the shelter that we would descend into a treacherous bog but almost immediately the walking improved as the ground was firm.

## The Cheviot

Leaving the warm embrace of Mounthooly bunkhouse, we climbed north west out of the valley on a well maintained path that slowly headed up to the western ridge, where it crossed the border fence and rejoined the Pennine Way.

Looking back into the valley, the peak of Cheviot is in the distance and below it is a forest, some of which is treasured ancient woodland. There is no path to it, or through it as it is a remnant that managed to survive due to the extreme remoteness of this part of the country. The trustees of College Valley are engaged in a long term project to revive and increase the amount of this precious woodland, something I can only applaud.

The paths in and out of College Valley were firm and well maintained, probably the best we'd encountered on the Cheviot Hills. The Pennine Way's habit is to weave through the bogs and soon we were struggling along once more. To the north, the valleys allowed tantalising glimpses of sunlit fertile fields stretching into the far distance. A sight that two thousand years ago had spurred the Romans to attempt to conquer the Picts.

As we descended the first farmhouse appeared, its sprawling yard oddly littered with old shipping containers. Beyond was a field where several emaciated elderly horses stood stock still, only their cloudy black eyes followed our passing.

Sunlit fertile fields and Kirk Yetholm below

The meanest hill of all rises up just before Kirk Yetholm. A severe incline that meant for a hundred yards or so we were puffing along. At the crest, finally we could see the little town sparkling in the sunshine due to a huge number of solar panels, which were an incongruous sight after the deluge of yesterday.

Chris recalled that there were wild raspberries in the hedgerow. This time, although we recognised the canes amongst the vegetation, the raspberries were long gone.

Meanwhile all appeared quiet in the little town, despite the world's press anxiously preparing their questions, hiding behind trees in readiness to doorstep us on our arrival. The ticker tape fireworks had been disguised amongst the litter bins and lorries thrummed gently in side streets as they tested the satellite links to world leaders, who were anxiously scanning the autocue to make sure they pronounced our names correctly. Somewhere over the North Sea, the Red Arrows were mustering in readiness for the *loop de loop* flypast.

Rather the reality was that at 12.15 on Friday 13$^{th}$ September 2019 to no fanfare whatsoever, two unremarkable old men walked across the green and sat down at a trestle table in the warm sunshine.

We had walked the Pennine Way.

Again.

On the next table were two walkers eating their lunch. They were on the St Cuthbert's Way and also had a terrible day yesterday. This was not a time for boastfulness or one-upmanship, so there was no swagger to our conversation.

Quietly we sat and reflected on how we felt all those years ago when we finally reached this point as peat-stained youngsters. I recall taking off my hated backpack and practically collapsing, as I do not believe I could have walked a step further that day. Although we were excited and elated to be finished, at the same time we had given every last ounce of our energy to the walk.

Today, I felt no tiredness but I did feel strangely hollow and in my heart I knew that finishing the walk was not a moment for elation. Already I missed the waking, packing, moving on and resting, the rhythms of the Pennine Way. All the moments that we had eagerly anticipated were gone and quickly they became an absence, an emptiness. The saving grace is that this is an emptiness that slowly fills again because mentally I will never stop walking the Way. Ever since

that day we finished so many years ago, the lonely hills have occupied a part of my mind and are always beckoning to me.

I took off my boots for the very last time. They did it, up to a point, although I might as well have been walking in my socks for the last two days for all the protection they afforded me. They should have finished their days in the boot graveyard at the gable end of the Border Hotel. However as I was less than delighted with their performance I had other plans for them.

## Das Boot

We both phoned home, to give them our news and let them know that we intended to get back this evening. Once inside the Border Hotel, we didn't ask for the free half pint offered, as Wainwright put it '*to bona fide walkers who have completed the walk in a single journey*' (this had been downgraded from a pint since 1979), nor do we require the signed certificate that they offer. We did not walk the Way for a free drink or a gaudy piece of paper. We are not Lightweights.

We know what we have done and do not seek or need the approval of others.

We ordered and paid for a well earned pint and bag of crisps and then sat outside opposite the green as the wind nipped at us. A small red car came to a halt and out came Helen and Stewart who have taken us entirely under their wing. We'd promised them lunch in return for a lift back to a train station, which as favours go was yet again very much in our favour. We settled down in the conservatory at the back of the Inn and ordered lunch. Helen and Stewart mentioned that they had anxiously watched the previous day's weather sweep over Haltwhistle and were happy that we had survived. I was also aware that they were watching us carefully, perhaps noticing that we were both strangely muted.

In order to change the mood I brought out my Pennine Way Companion to read page 4, 'The End' aloud. It is a moving piece, intended to be read only by those who have completed the Way. With extraordinary prescience Wainwright managed to encapsulate the forty years of thoughts and feelings that should be welling up inside me and I did find my voice faltering as I said the words. At the same time, deep down I sensed an absence of emotion.

I know that when it comes to the Pennine Way other more modern guidebooks are available (which even acknowledge that both sexes can walk the Way). As I see it, when I walk with Wainwright, I am accompanying the king of fell-walking. He may not have wanted to share the walk with me or any other walker but there is a warmth and beauty to his books that I have not found in other guides.

We collected our belongings and like forty years ago we had our picture taken outside at the gable end of the Border Hotel. The drive back to Newcastle took a surprisingly long time as we hit heavy commuter traffic on the way to the station.

All the words that we used to express our gratitude felt deficient in the face of the incredible kindness that we'd experienced. We stood at the station drop-off point and watched as they edged the car onto the slip road that joined the traffic jam and at this moment I felt for my wallet. It wasn't where I expected it to be. The little red car was close to joining the main road and I ran as fast as I could to catch up with it before they nosed into the Friday evening traffic. To their great surprise I pulled open the back door and apologising profusely,

**Opposite: the finish line, then and now**

BORDER HOTEL
END OF PENNINE WAY
The Border hotel
end of the Pennine Way

reclaimed the wallet that I'd left on the back seat. I thanked them once more and limped back to Chris. My unexpected sprint had strained a calf muscle.

We had about half an hour until our train arrived so we stocked up on sandwiches and drinks. A glance at the arrivals board showed that the train was running twenty minutes late. The ticket that we'd bought was cheap because it was a split ticket that had three changes before we arrived at Audley End, (which is the nearest station to Chris's house) and each of these changes was timed pretty tightly. If we missed a connection, the ticket was probably invalid for the next train. I decided I was better off not looking too closely at the terms and conditions.

The first train arrived and it took us to York. The on-board announcer apologised for the late running but did not suggest that any effort was going to be made to make up the time. It was a fraught journey and we arrived at York five minutes after our connection. Despite my aching calf muscle I ran across the bridge to the platform which I could see was empty of people and as I got closer I could make out the display board. It stated that this train was also running late and was not due for a few more minutes. It was headed for Stevenage, which at least would put us within driving distance should the worst happen and we get stuck there.

We headed south as golden sunlight shafted across the newly harvested fields. Again there was no effort to catch up on the lost time, so we arrived in darkness at Stevenage a good half an hour after our connection. Fortunately, we breezed through the station unchallenged and caught the next Cambridge train, again arriving half an hour later than our original timetable. Here we crossed the platform for the Audley End train. As journeys go, we were grateful to be home and to have paid less than half the scheduled fare but we could have done without the extra excitement.

The brightly lit platform was empty and we found Mag and Sylvie walking and talking in the dark car park. It was a relief for Mag to finally be reunited with Chris after all that had happened in the family since he left. I too was looking forward to being home but it was tinged with sadness because our long-planned adventure was over.

I hugged Sylvie tightly as she sceptically inspected my nascent beard, then I placed my backpack in the boot and got into the driver's seat.

'Well, how was it?' she asked.

# Email

**From**: Robin Kane

**Subject**: 40 years later.

Hi Duncan and Chris,

Congratulations, you are awe inspiring!
It's not so much the hike as the fact that 40 years later, two friends embarked on an Odyssey into their past and, while I suspect there were some challenges, achieved something momentous.

I admire the friendship and the accomplishment.

It was such a pleasure meeting you and it made my hike much better for the experience.

Take care,
Robin

**The view from the tent on a practise walk**

# Chapter 20
## Frayed ends

**Duncan:** Occasionally I find myself daydreaming about what my parents were doing at my age. In my case it's a simple calculation because my father was forty years older than me. So looking back, I can calculate that when I was walking into Kirk Yetholm on the 3rd September 1979 my father at this age and date was sitting in the back of a lorry being taken off for basic training. He had determined that he wanted to be a pilot in the event of war as he had heard the stories about the trenches in the Great War and decided that wasn't for him. In 1938 he joined the Civil Air Guard taking classes in theory and practice of flight and even had a couple of flights in a trainer.

Then Germany invaded Poland and he decided on the 2nd September 1939 (the day before the war started) to sign up at the Air Ministry in Whitehall. On the threshold of which he was firmly rebuffed by two air men.

'We don't need pilots. Go home and wait until you are called up.'

Just as he was leaving he noticed there was a queue next door. The recruiting sergeant in charge asked him if he was any of these trades, while pointing at a chalkboard covered in crafts. Dad was an electrician and so by this happy accident he enlisted as RAF ground crew and thereby greatly improved his chances of surviving the war.

If we roll on forty years, you can see that my Dad would be the same age as I am now, and I would like to think that he would have been more impressed by our second attempt as there wasn't much in the way of whelm the first time we completed the Way. Not that he was dismissive of it but maybe the next few paragraphs will explain.

Forty years before, on my return to home I knew that the Pennine Way had changed me in a number of ways. Physically in sixteen days I had somehow managed to lose an astonishing stone and half (21lb or

10kg), which since I was already very lean at the start made me look like a walking skeleton for a few months. It is not as if we starved ourselves but walking with a full pack uses up a lot of calories.

The real change was inside. The previous year of my life had been a tremendous disappointment to me and I expect to my parents as well. Having spent three years studying photography I had managed to get a job in a small high street photographic firm and although I had no expectations of massive wealth (the first few years of being a photographic assistant are poorly paid even in the best of places) I was troubled to find that I had no enthusiasm for taking pictures for other people. I liked photography, I still do, just not as a commercial activity, which was a problem if I wanted to eat and pay rent. I could have carried on with it and maybe I would have found the spark to reignite my interest but I was disillusioned and needed to find a place to rebuild.

Chris had told me about a job at St Bartholomew's Hospital for an audiovisual technician. I had no idea what it entailed but the main attraction for me was that under no circumstances would I be required to take photographs. In fact the contract expressly forbade it.

When we completed the Pennine Way the next summer, it began the rebuilding of my inner confidence. So that when the television unit at Bart's reformed a year or so later, I found my way to it and from there I rekindled the spark of creativity that I thought I had lost forever.

It is easy to spot the threads of a life story from a distance but back then I felt like a frayed end that had completely wasted the previous five years on a foolish ambition.

What about now, how do I feel today after our successful return to the Way? Physically again I lost some weight, just over half a stone, returning to a weight that I have not seen since we began the Way forty years ago. It just goes to show that pork scratchings can be part of a weight-loss regime.

Then there is the fate of my boots. I took them back to the shop and practically the whole staff of this warehouse operation came out to take a look. I argued that a pair of walking boots should be able to survive the first forty-five days of its life. I had only taken them for a walk after all, and with less than two hundred miles on the clock the soles were gaping and letting in water. I had to admit that there was fire damage but the only reason for that was because I was trying to mend the soles. The fire damage was not the reason for my complaint.

Some of them questioned that such a 'lightweight boot' was up to the rigours of the Pennine Way. I countered by reminding them that I had bought the boot on the recommendation of one their staff (who was not present). After they had recovered from the initial shock of my boots' appearance it was grudgingly admitted that they should have performed better and I was offered a replacement. With mixed feelings I had to give the remains back so that the manufacturer could 'learn' from them, although I now realise I really didn't want to keep a pair of rotten old boots.

How did the two walks compare? Overall, was one walk better than the other?

Take the weather for example. This is very important as to how the walk is experienced and without doubt it was much colder and wetter the second time around. On the first occasion after the deluge that stranded us in Malham it was pretty warm for the rest of the walk. On both occasions we had excellent conditions for the High Cup day, which is the one day - more than any other - that most benefits from a view. But overall the weather was better the first time, so that has to be a mark for the first walk.

The equipment seemed to be more robust forty years ago. Our tent was much stronger and other pieces of kit were built to last. Whereas this modern kit seems to wear out in front of my eyes. Has the last 40 years of innovation mainly led to cheap and flimsy rubbish? However there were some successes on the second occasion. My rucksack was in a different league and exceeded all my expectations - mind you it was in a different league to the other backpacks in the shop. As were my waterproof trousers. My legs did get cold but they were never wet. I should make special mention of my Bridgedale socks which were not only made in Britain but they were the most comfortable walking socks (and probably the most expensive) that I've ever worn. Worth every penny, though. The sleeping pad which was inflated with only nine or ten breaths did allow me to sleep on my side and isolate me from the ground. That's evens I think.

The terrain is just so different now with so much of the Way covered in flagstones. Back then, walking through peat was very arduous but the times recorded in our Wainwrights suggest that we covered the miles faster on the peat than we did on the flagstones. In fact we were genuinely in awe of our younger selves on several of the days. However we did notice on the second occasion when we walked across peat that if it was not too waterlogged then it was a lot easier to walk on. And I think it was a fairly dry summer forty years ago which leads me to conclude that it is evens again.

Route finding using the mobile phone and apps was a vast improvement on using a map and compass. I genuinely feel sorry for anyone who is still relying on map technology today. That's a mark for the second walk.

Totting that up the points tally is evens and I guess I have the deciding vote. So, if I was to rate which walk was more difficult then, to the dismay of modern day walkers, my opinion is that it was plain sailing the second time around. It was still a massive challenge for us 'old men of the Way' but somehow it was always within our abilities. As we walked the miles we recognised that it was much more arduous in almost every way forty years ago.

**Chris**: Duncan's summation is spot on. Sitting on the green at Kirk Yetholm for the second time, it felt good. I felt good. I felt stronger, less tired and more sorry to be leaving the walk than I did the first time. Apart from yesterday's experience of the Cheviots, the unpleasantness of which was really entirely due to the weather, I don't feel like I was especially challenged over the sixteen days. We can argue why that might be, and the two of us may well go over it during many miles of walking still to come, but I think it was mainly down to choosing not to camp, and thereby resting properly most nights. The cumulative effect of two weeks of bad nights in the tent could well have done for our second Pennine Way attempt: it certainly would have made it far less enjoyable. Of course our extensive preparation and the flagstones played significant parts in our success too, but that success shows clearly that mere age is not a barrier to such achievements. I hope that this description of our second completion of this great walk will help others believe that there's no reason they can't do it too, and give it a go.

Not much more than twenty four hours after we bade farewell to Mounthooly, I was walking again, strolling the three quarters of a mile to the supermarket to do the daily shop. Real life. There were still some arrangements for the funeral, now just a few days away, to be worked out; catering to order, final decisions about music and flowers to be made. I also had a day's work (mercifully just the one as it turned out) at the hospital in the meantime. The Pennines already seemed a thousand miles away, the Way something we'd walked in another lifetime - well, two other lifetimes.

Just as Wainwright predicted, nobody was interested in hearing about what I'd been up to for the last three weeks. Even neighbour Tony, himself an intrepid outdoor type who I'm sure would love to know about the famous long distance path, appeared to have forgotten that I'd even been away, and to this day we still haven't talked about it. I guessed that at least at the funeral I'd have Pennine Way conversations, as family and friends at the reception struggled for small talk, but no more than a few sentences on the subject were exchanged. At work I looked for opportunities to engage patients in conversation about our recent trip: 'Have you been away this year? I've just walked the Pennine Way!' - but without success.

Maybe that's how it should be. For Duncan and I though, as we continue to walk the footpaths of Essex and Suffolk our memories of the sixteen days - and the forty years! - provide the basis for many a conversation. We are bound together by our shared experience, our friendship strengthened and deepened by what we did together.

**Duncan:** We walk, we reminisce and talk of the future, of places and paths old and new that we will tread together.

Chris & Duncan

Border

The view from Slioch
- a vast rugged emptiness

# And finally

**Duncan:** Back in 1980 after our successful completion of the Pennine Way, I wanted to walk the West Highland Way which was officially opening that year. Being half-Scottish I have always been drawn to the lofty mountains of the Highlands.

I had seen the western Highlands while on a biology field trip during sixth form. The field trip centre was situated at the south easterly end of Loch Maree near Kinlochewe and as well as standing on the sides of the mountains doing surveys of bog plants and wading through Loch Torridon identifying kelp and marine animals, we also took a day off and climbed Slioch. A mighty standalone Munro that dominates the Loch Maree eastern bank.

It was a long climb to the summit on that clear sunny day. To the south west of us, the only road in sight was a thin black shoelace that snaked up the side of the Loch. The view to the north east was of deep lochs and barren mountainside, a vast rugged emptiness fading into the hazy blue distance that pulled at me.

A year later in between school and poly I went on a YHA guided walking holiday that was grandly titled 'In the steps of the '45' and visited many of the places in the Scottish Highlands that played a part in the Jacobite rebellion.

Starting at Inverness we walked the boggy battlefield of Culloden and followed Bonnie Prince Charlie's escape to the Isles, passing several famous and some more minor sites that were involved in the story of the rebellion. Along the way we climbed Ben Nevis on a grey dismal day which had none of the joy of climbing Slioch.

In the West Highland museum at Fort William we saw the secret portrait of Bonnie Prince Charlie and other artefacts from the Jacobite rebellion. Later, we visited the moving Glenfinnan monument on Loch Shiel where the Young Pretender raised his Royal Standard and began the rebellion. Nearby we were led to a cave where the fleeing Prince was supposed to have taken shelter, before finally being rowed across to Skye and exile. (One of many apparently, as there's barely a hole in the ground around here that doesn't claim this particular honour.)

We had arrived at the tiny fishing port of Mallaig which is where the history tour ended. We were booked onto a Caledonian MacBrayne ferry that chugged up the sound to Kyle.

This is a journey that is seared into my memory. Skye and the shadowy rugged peaks of the Cuillins to the west glistened in the afternoon sunshine and to the east, the mainland, like the view from the top of Slioch, a vast wilderness that captivated me once more.

The next few days were the most spectacular; the Five Sisters of Kintail, a dramatic and dizzying ridge walk (which regretfully I had to sit out as I had a cold), then up through Glen Affric to stay at one of the most remote youth hostels in Britain, before finally returning to Inverness.

I was anxious to see this landscape once more but for some reason Chris was not to be charmed by these tales as he seemed to be reticent about venturing to the Highlands. So it was that a compromise was made and we plumped for something completely different instead.

**Chris:** As ever, my memory of things that took place forty years ago is found wanting. I don't recall Duncan's expression of his need to revisit what is by his and everyone else's accounts a spectacularly beautiful place. I'm also a bit baffled to think I wouldn't have gone along with it.

I am clear that the West Highland Way has drifted through conversations in more recent times. I have been left with the belief that while Duncan thinks it's a wonderful and beautiful part of the world, he also thinks that it always rains, visibility is often poor so you might not even see the grandeur of the place, there are midges, there's a lack of comfortable accommodation so a consequent possibility of needing to camp and that on balance he'd choose *not* to undertake the ninety odd miles. As a result of that knowledge, I can't say I've ever researched the walk, or even know where it is. Until today that is, and I can't be more straightforward than this: if he wants to do the West Highland Way, he can count me in. We might even write a book: *The West Highland Way: two even older friends get wet in Scotland*. How does that sound? Reader: watch this space.

# Acknowledgements

Firstly we must thank our wives and families for all their support, before, during and after the walk.

Then there are those people who helped us complete the Way. To James who persuaded his parents Stewart and Helen to put us up for one night. For Stewart and Helen to actively volunteer to do it again the next evening and finally insist on meeting us at Kirk Yetholm to drive us to Newcastle train station, well, there aren't words.

Charlene from Mounthooly deserves special mention for going above and beyond her role without expecting any reward.

Andy and Barbara who kindly drove us to Edale and Bernard and Linda who met us in Hebden Bridge and offered to take Chris back if things changed.

The 'interloper,' Jerome, who endured terrible weather on the Way while suffering job uncertainty. He kept his job in the end if you were concerned to know how that panned out. Jerome lifted our spirits and made the Malham to Horton day much more bearable.

The cohort who shared part or all of our journey, some whose names we have either forgotten or were never exchanged such as the young(er) couple, the older couple, and the father and son partnership - I hope they are still on course. Rob, the intrepid veteran athlete, Robin the American walker and of course the *Keeper of the Rules of the Pennine Way,* Simon and his partner Wendy.

Thanks also to James, Jerome and Roger van Schaick for permission to use their photographs in the book. Special mention must go to Jonathan Theobald for combing through the text and pointing out errors and inconsistencies. Those that are still there are all of our own making.

Much in the same way that we didn't want the Pennine Way to end, it has also been difficult to complete this book … but the memories, they will linger.

# Just one more thing

Since you've come this far maybe you'd be interested to hear about *Masked, the unbelievable Harry Bensley.*

I first read about Harry in an article published in my local newspaper. It told the story of a mystery man who ended up in Essex. It was claimed that when he was younger he was the subject of a wager to walk round the world. The condition that made this wager stand out was that he had to remain anonymous until the walk was complete and in order to do this he wore a knight's helmet. The wager was for an eye-watering sum, equivalent to nearly seven million pounds in today's money and the actual attempt was well documented in contemporaneous newspaper reports.

Sadly he failed but not before he had walked a very long way. The reason he was unable to complete the walk was because, he said, the outbreak of the Great War made the final countries he had to walk across out of bounds. He returned to Britain and joined the army.

It was quite a tale and I put the article to one side because I wanted to find out more when I had a little spare time. That spare time suddenly became all of my spare time as I uncovered a mountain of fascinating information. It felt as though Harry had walked off the page and into my life and was not to be satisfied until I had told his story. The Harry Bensley I found was famous, even notorious, not once but twice and managed to completely re-invent himself three times. His life story is truly unbelievable and this book is the first to give it a proper airing.

Available as a paperback: ISBN 978-1-9162174-0-9
Or an eBook: ISBN 978-1-9162174-1-6

When he lived in Wivenhoe he was a changed man
Just how much he had changed was more than anyone knew

# Masked

## The unbelievable Harry Bensley

Duncan Say

www.ingramcontent.com/pod-product-compliance
Ingram Content Group UK Ltd.
Pitfield, Milton Keynes, MK11 3LW, UK
UKHW062305290726
14090UKWH00018B/888